THE ART OF AGILE PRODUCT OWNERSHIP

A GUIDE FOR PRODUCT MANAGERS, BUSINESS ANALYSTS, AND ENTREPRENEURS

Allan Kelly

Apress®

The Art of Agile Product Ownership: A Guide for Product Managers, Business Analysts, and Entrepreneurs

Allan Kelly
London, UK

ISBN-13 (pbk): 978-1-4842-5167-6   ISBN-13 (electronic): 978-1-4842-5168-3
https://doi.org/10.1007/978-1-4842-5168-3

Managing Director, Apress Media LLC: Welmoed Spahr
Acquisitions Editor: Shiva Ramachandran
Development Editor: Rita Fernando
Coordinating Editor: Rita Fernando

Cover designed by eStudioCalamar

Distributed to the book trade worldwide by Springer Science+Business Media New York, 233 Spring Street, 6th Floor, New York, NY 10013. Phone 1-800-SPRINGER, fax (201) 348-4505, e-mail orders-ny@springer-sbm.com, or visit www.springeronline.com. Apress Media, LLC is a California LLC and the sole member (owner) is Springer Science + Business Media Finance Inc (SSBM Finance Inc). SSBM Finance Inc is a **Delaware** corporation.

For information on translations, please e-mail rights@apress.com, or visit http://www.apress.com/rights-permissions.

Apress titles may be purchased in bulk for academic, corporate, or promotional use. eBook versions and licenses are also available for most titles. For more information, reference our Print and eBook Bulk Sales web page at http://www.apress.com/bulk-sales.

Any source code or other supplementary material referenced by the author in this book is available to readers on GitHub via the book's product page, located at www.apress.com/9781484251676. For more detailed information, please visit http://www.apress.com/source-code.

Printed on acid-free paper

Contents

Part IV: Challenges

About the Author

Allan Kelly still considers himself a software engineer—even if nobody pays him to code any more. Deciding what to build, understanding customer needs, designing the software, and organizing the processes are all part of software engineering to him.

He helps companies and teams undertake software engineering using agile techniques working as a consultant, coach, or manager. Most of his clients are small innovative companies few people have heard of. His better known clients include Virgin Atlantic, Qualcomm, the Bank of England, Reed Elsevier, and Swift.

Allan has pioneered techniques such as Value Poker, Time-Value Profiles, and Retrospective Dialogue Sheets. He is the author of the perennial essay "Dear Customer, the Truth about IT" and a number of books, including *Continuous Digital*, *A Little Book of Requirements and User Stories*, *Xanpan*, and *Business Patterns for Software Developers*.

Contact: allan@allankelly.net

Twitter: @allankellynet

Web site and blog: www.allankellyassociates.co.uk/blog/

Acknowledgments

Many thanks to all the Product Owners, Product Managers, Business Analysts, Systems Analysts, Business Partners, and Requirements Engineers to have helped me understand the many varied ways companies answer the "what are we building?" question.

Prologue

George Hunter, Product Owner

Wednesday. George was the Tactical Product Owner, TPO, for the Cell Optimizer product. Project managers and operations staff regularly called him to discuss what Cell Optimizer could do and whether it would be useful for their work. In addition to answering their questions, he took notes on both how the product would help their project and how it could help them even more—whether by adding new features, enhancing existing features, improving performance, accuracy, ease of use, or one of a multitude of other attributes.

Most of George's day was spent working with his technical team. Every second week they would hold a planning meeting. Today was the day before the planning meeting which meant George needed to comb through his product backlog and quarter plan to select the stories he wanted the team to tackle. Some of the stories he already knew could be broken down—these were Epics—but the team always surprised him in finding interesting ways to break down what he thought was a small story into several smaller stories.

Normally he would sit down with Diana for a few hours during the backlog review, or at least the tip of top of the backlog. Diana was the Strategic Product Owner—or SPO—and also the R&D Centre chief. But this week Diana was in Dubai with clients and operations staff. Although he called her a couple of times to discuss stories, he made most of the decisions himself knowing she had delegated authority to him.

As he worked through his backlog and plans, he occasionally wondered over to see Ahmed, the technical lead. There had been a time when the whole team would be involved in reviewing the backlog, but over time some of the team complained that it was a waste of time. So, the team deputized Ahmed to attend the meeting; then Ahmed decided George could just ask him as needed. Tomorrow's planning meeting offered plenty of time for technical conversations after all.

By the time he got on the tram to travel home, he was confident he had enough stories and jobs selected to keep the team busy, and a few more in case they were ready to stretch.

The next day, **Thursday**, started with a 90-minute demonstration of the work which had been completed during the previous two weeks. George already knew what the demo would contain as he had previewed and approved everything during the sprint. He could have done the demo himself, but he knew it was good to let Programmers and Testers show off their own work.

Most of the audience was Project Managers who wanted to use Cell Optimizer on their own projects. They were joined by some of the staff who would be hands-on with the product plus Product Owners and technical staff from other product streams which worked alongside Cell Optimizer.

Diana dialed in as did some operations Project Managers and other staff throughout the world. Occasionally one of the regional CxOs would too, especially if a high-profile project was involved.

He was on hand to discuss questions from the audience and take more notes on how they would like the product to evolve—plus pick up whispers of new projects which might want to hire Cell Optimizer.

The demo went off without a hitch—which didn't always happen—and the team was clear to deploy the new software. While the rest of the team grabbed a coffee, Darren, the DevOps lead, would push the button to deploy Cell Optimizer to AWS. Later he would cut CDs to send to those who needed an on premise install. Not every user installed the latest version, but the team would only support the latest version, so the first thing anyone who had a problem needed to do was upgrade their software.

After coffee the team went into a retrospective for an hour and a half. The important thing was to find two or three things the team could improve. They didn't need to be the best ideas—although that helped, they didn't need to argue, they just needed a couple of things which had the potential to improve performance by 1%. And if they tried something and it didn't help, then they simply undid the change.

The planning meeting finally happened after lunch. The first task was to clear down the board of all the work done and update the tracking graphs. With that done the team lead stepped back and George stepped to forward. He quickly outlined what he was aiming for in the next sprint and then laid out the stories he was requesting.

The team moved through the stories in priority order. One by one the team looked at the story, discussed what was wanted with George, rewrote the story, added acceptance criteria, and in many cases broke the story down into several smaller stories which George either kept in the sprint or pushed back to a later sprint. Often the team members broke stories down into technical tasks they needed to complete; this was more an act of collective design than work packaging.

It was only at this stage did the team add any effort estimates to the stories and tasks. Cell Optimizer was a little unusual here; most teams estimated three months' worth of stories into the future. The Cell Optimizer team used to do this, but they found that they spent a lot of time estimating work which never actually got scheduled, so they calculated an average and told George to assume every story was four days' work. Surprisingly this worked quite well, sometimes it was massively over and sometimes massively under, but eight out of ten times it worked well.

By the time the planning meeting was over, it was time to go home. George put in a quick call to Diana to update her on outcomes, but there was nothing unexpected, so the call was short.

Right after the stand-up meeting on **Friday**, George set about updating his quarter plan and backlog to reflect the outcome of the planning meeting. But he didn't get very far.

First of all, team members wanted to talk about the stories that were to be done. That was quite normal, stories are placeholders for a conversation after all, and talking about them was a big part of George's job. Some of these conversations happened right away, but most of them were scheduled as 3-Amigos sessions to occur over the remainder of the week.

But, second, George was interrupted by a request from the field. Cell Optimizer wasn't producing the expected result in Egypt, and someone needed to investigate. George wrote out a yellow card—urgent but unplanned—and went to Ahmed, the technical lead. They looked at the request together, rewrote the card, and Ahmed set about doing it. As technical lead, Ahmed was usually the one to pick up urgent but unplanned work. Not always though, others could be called on too.

All in all, George hadn't finished his own updates by the close of business. And he was due at a conference in town on Monday—inconvenient because the team had lots of questions, but missing the conference would both deprive him of the latest thinking in the field and the chance to meet end-users.

So, although he shouldn't have, George ended up working through the backlog and plan changes over the weekend.

Most of **Monday's** conference was boring, nothing new, but a few side conversations gave George new perspectives on customer needs. One of the presentations was from a direct competitor, while it didn't contain any revelations it was reassuring to know what they were thinking along the same lines. But then again, when he thought about it: Diana always said she didn't want to get into feature shoot-outs. She wanted Cell Optimizer to differentiate, perhaps tackle the same customer job, but help the client achieve the same end differently, better.

It was **Tuesday** before he got to sit down properly with Diana and find out what had happened in Dubai. She had decided that George should do the Dubai trip next month; she said this was because George would benefit from seeing Cell Optimizer in the wild and meeting with the project team, but he suspected she was simply fed up of traveling.

Diana had come back with some more ideas and perspectives around Jobs to be Done by Cell Optimizer—or JTBD as they usually called them. (Diana and George had an ongoing debate as to whether Cell Optimizer provided several mechanisms to help with one job to be done or whether it helped with several jobs to be done which all centered around optimizing the cell. Either way George had long ago given up on the idea that one day they would be "done." No matter how many stories they delivered to improve the "one" job to be done, they could always see more to do. Although that didn't stop people asking, "When will you be done?")

Despite George needing to spend time with the technical team, she thought they should take a couple of hours on **Wednesday** to revise the roadmap. The roadmap wasn't due for a full review until next month—another daylong session—but she wanted to review it in light of the Dubai trip. Diana couldn't do it there and then because she had to see the COO later on Tuesday, so Wednesday afternoon was marked for the roadmap review.

George could have ducked out, but Diana and he were proud of their shared vision and the ability to deputize for one another. One or two of the other teams had TPOs who didn't work as closely with their SPO, and there were occasional tensions when they wanted different things. Diana knew that George and the technical team could see things the technology could do that she had no idea about. In fact, Diana herself was SPO for three "Cell" teams at her center, and there was some tension with TPO for the Cell Monitor product.

Part of Diana's urgently in reviewing the roadmap was because **Thursday** was capacity planning day. Since they introduced capacity planning, a lot of the pressure had come off the roadmap. In his previous job George forced the roadmap to be part of the vision statement, a thinking tool, a capacity plan, and a series of promises to projects and stakeholders. Now the roadmap was a what-if thinking tool to elaborate on the vision and imagine the future, while the capacity plan allowed medium-term promises to be made to projects. One was vision, the other was delivery.

Although Diana was SPO for three products at her center, she didn't have the final say on resourcing. So, in capacity planning, a couple of senior Project Managers and account managers joined to form a Centre Portfolio board which met quarterly.

Thursday found George and two other TPOs presenting their product lists to the Centre Portfolio board and make their bids for resources. The portfolio board had no time for effort estimates—occasionally new staff would present effort estimates as part of their bid only to be knocked back.

The portfolio board looked at capacity—how many man-days the teams had over the next six months—and the value, or other priority, of the proposed Jobs to be Done for projects over that period. First off, the portfolio board looked at all the jobs to be done and ranked them by value and priority. Immediately some fell off the end, and some unlucky operations Project Managers would have to be told their request were not going to happen, they would have to use the product as they were.

Next the portfolio board allocated man-days against each JTBD and determined the priority order. Some jobs were small but would be done soon; others were large but would wait their turn. It hadn't always been this way. For years teams, Project Managers, and TPOs had argued over effort estimates. It took time to realize that business need and value should be the driver.

The second thing which changed the approach was when teams could reliably demo working, deliverable, software every second week. Once a team is potentially done every second week, the game changes.

Each team is tasked with work and told: "You can give 20%"—or whatever—"of your time over the next six months to this job. It needs to be in the field by …"—some date—"how you achieve that is up to you and the TPO." Giving the teams objectives rather than details, real deadlines instead of repeating their effort estimates back to them and trusting them to deliver something was a game changer.

Although each of the three product teams would remain largely the same, it was normal that a few people moved between teams. Sometimes this was a matter of expediency—Cell Optimizer was relatively well staffed, while Cell Monitor was struggling—it also reflected individuals' requests to move teams.

All in all, that was Thursday. George was glad for a **Friday** where he got to spend time with the team, hold some 3-Amigos sessions to flesh out acceptance criteria, review some screen changes, do some tests, update his product backlog and quarter plan after the capacity planning session, and reply to some user questions and more Project Manager enquiries.

Mondays come around quickly, and despite a busy Friday, George hadn't had a chance to catch up with himself—and team members had more questions and items for review. Monday morning provided some time, but shortly after lunch, he was on the way to the airport. **Tuesday** was a client site visit and a flight back.

All of a sudden it was **Wednesday** again, and George had to review his back-log and get ready for Thursday's planning meeting. Since Diana was in the office, he wanted to spend some time with her talking about what the team would do next. And needless the end of the sprint means the usual end-of-spring story reviews and sign-offs, a little more testing and suggesting some final modifications before the demon tomorrow.

Was it really two weeks since the last demo? Retrospective? And planning? Well at least the next two weeks wouldn't be so busy, no conference, no customer visit, no capacity planning, George would get to really get ahead of the game. Good thing too because the following sprint he'd be out in Dubai for a week. "Normal" weeks were not very common really.

Day	Theme	AM	PM
Wednesday	Get ready for planning	With team	Backlog review
Thursday	End/start of print	Demo and retrospective	Sprint planning
Friday	With team	Team conversations, support	Quarter plan
Monday	Conference		
Tuesday	Diana sync	Backlog review, plan review, JTBD, etc.	
Wednesday	Roadmap		
Thursday	Capacity planning		
Friday	With team	Team conversations, feature reviews	ACs, stories, etc.
Monday	With team	Team conversations	Flight to client
Tuesday	Client	Client meeting	Flight back

... and repeat.

From time to time, George was called by recruiters. He had a good reputation and people often suggested him, but, despite all the hassles here, and despite never having enough time, he liked it here. He always wondered what it would be like working elsewhere. After all, in Scrum books Product Owners never had to go to industry conferences, or Dubai. In those books people seemed to have enough time; they didn't have to respond to field requests, attend portfolio boards, work with an SPO, or half the other things he did. Was there something he was missing?

Introduction

The Product Owner role is the most critical role in an agile team. It is also the most difficult role to fill well. In part, it is difficult because the demands on the Product Owner are so diverse and the expectations of co-workers so varied.

Product Owner can be a lonely role—there is normally one per team—but it need not be. While the Product Owner is the decision maker and a specialist in understanding the demands on the product, they are a team member too. While their role differs from most other teammates, the whole team succeeds or fails together. The team members are there to help the Product Owner—just as the Product Owner is there to help the team. Just because there is one designated Product Owner does not mean others cannot help. Indeed, the more members of the team who appreciate the nature of product ownership, the more the team can help.

Many new Product Owners look for a framework to describe what they should be doing and to tell them what steps to take each day. Those who look will find matrices, wheels, checklists, certifications, and more. But in truth none of these are completely satisfying.

For the fact is, product ownership is an art not a science. Every Product Owner is an individual, and the environment they work in will be different to any other. An ideal framework for one may say little for another. One cannot write down a single, reusable, recipe for all Product Owners.

Sure, the objectives of all Product Owner are pretty much the same: *create and ship great products which bring delight to customers*. Yet there is no fixed way of doing that. While there are common techniques and similarities in how Product Owners work, and especially in how they work with teams, there are differences too.

Some Product Owners sit side-by-side with the delivery team; others sit on the opposite side of the world.

Some Product Owners create products for the mass market, products you can buy online or buy in the supermarket. Others create products for one very special customer.

Some Product Owners must carry the full workload by themselves. Others can share the workload with specialists—Product Managers, Business Analysts, and User Experience Designers, for example. Product ownership is often vested in one person, the Product Owner, but it need not be. Ownership of the product can be shared—even if one person retains final decision-making authority.

Teams without a Product Owner need to ask themselves: *Would the team, and the end product, be better if there were a Product Owner?*

The majority of teams are better off with a Product Owner although effective teams do exist which lack a Product Owner. Let me suggest that such teams either exist in an unusual environment or the duties normally filled by a Product Owner are being undertaken by other team members. As such *product ownership* is being practiced—market research is being done, customers are being consulted, work is being prioritized, and so on—it is just that the team has distributed this work in a different way.

Teams which practice product ownership without a dedicated Product Owner still need to consider the issues discussed in this book, for example: *Is enough time being given to customer understanding? Are features being evaluated post release?* Even without a Product Owner, there is a need for product ownership.

Almost all Product Owners work in an agile environment, but some environments are more agile than others. Many are in a constant state of change—either because the organization is still on a journey to become agile, or because having become agile the culture of continual improvement keeps things changing.

The question

Once you accept that product ownership is an art not a science, it is natural to see the Product Owner as an artist who must create their own answer.

In this book I aim to help Product Owners create their own answer to the question:

> *What is the best way for me to fill the Product Owner role?*

Part 1 looks at why we have Product Owners and the parameters they work within. Part 2 looks at what Product Owners do and considers what they should not do. Part 3 takes a different approach and considers related roles. These roles predate the Product Owner role and overlap with the role. Finally, part 4 looks at some of the challenges facing POs and suggests some solutions.

Product Ownership beyond software

One last note before I begin properly. This book considers Product Owners and product ownership in the context of software—software products and technology. As more and more industries become digital, the work in these industries looks more like software development. It is unsurprising then that agile is spreading from software development into other domains and industries.

So, while I say little about product ownership in other domains—marketing, finance, construction, to name a few—I expect some readers will come from those domains. Right now, mid-2019, I don't believe I, or anyone else for that matter, has seen enough product ownership beyond software development to really discuss how it differs. Undoubtedly there will be much in common, but there will also be differences.

From what I have seen of agile in non-software domains, I would suggest that while product ownership remains valuable, there may be less need for dedicated Product Owners. The boundary between Product Owner (the specialist in demands) and the delivery team (specialists in building and delivering products) is less distinct; there is more crossover.

Another reason why the need for a Product Owners may be reduced is that many non-software domains do not suffer from the same difficulty in agreeing "what are we building." This is particularly true when agile style working is applied in places with more routine and less innovation. In such places there is less difficulty in deciding what gets done and what gets left undone.

Similarly, software development has traditionally adopted the project model. This model forces questions such as *What will be built? How much will it cost? When will it be done?* to the fore. While used in other domains projects are not universal. Indeed this author has himself argued that the project model is a poor fit for software development and destroys value.[1]

Secondly, the technology demands on software professionals means they are largely cut off from customers. Sometimes because of the client-supplier relationship, or because of the deep focus and technical knowledge software development demands, software professionals often lack opportunities, and skills, to speak to customers. Consequently, software teams need Product Owners as specialists in "what to build"—and specifically "what to build next." This is not necessarily the case in domains where there is more customer contact. Consequently, it is easier to distribute product ownership around the team.

---

[1] Allan Kelly, *Project Myopia* (Software Strategy Ltd / LeanPub, 2018).

Still, teams outside of software might want to ask themselves: *Would we benefit from a Product Owner? And what would that Product Owner do?*

Hopefully, as experience grows, a clearer picture of product ownership outside the software domain will emerge. And then it might be time to bring those lessons back to software development and reconsider the Product Owner role in software teams.

Meet the Product Owner

"If we're going to make this decision based on opinions, we're going to use my opinion."

—Jim Barksdale, CEO of Netscape Communications[1]

Every Product Owner is different. Every Product Owner needs to work out what is right the right way for them to fill the Product Owner role. Every organization is different. Every team is different, and every individual is different.

For a newly appointed Product Owner, the first job is to sit down and decide what type of Product Owner they will be. Both what the organization expects of them and what type of Product Owner they want to be. For example:

- They may be a *Backlog Administrator* taking instructions from others, structuring and filtering the backlog, working effectively with the team, and *burning down the backlog*.

- They may be a *Subject Matter Expert* using expert knowledge of the domain to decide what the right product to build is, then helping team members understand the details of what is being built.

---

[1] Quoted in Marty Cagan, *Inspired: How to Create Products Customers Love* (SVPG Press, 2008).

- Some Product Owners will work like *Business Analysts*. They will analyze internal process and business lines, meet with stakeholders, and balance competing internal requests. Frequently they will work as proxy customers.

- Others Product Owners will need to get out on the road. They will meet with customers—and potential customers. They will study their market and seek out opportunities using the skills of *Product Management*.

All Product Owners will need to call on skills from other fields too: Project Management, Consulting, and Entrepreneurship, to name a few.

Every organization will—rightly or wrongly—expect different things from the people it anoints Product Owner.

I cannot give you a flow chart for what a Product Owner does or should do. Nor can I give you a set of rules to say, "When the customer says Foo the Product Owner should do Bar." In the language of business schools, there is no contingent way of being a Product Owner. Every Product Owner and organization is different, and they need to find their own path.

Product Owners do not work in isolation; they are the first and foremost members of a team charged with creating and delivering products and/or services—typically software development teams. They will be members of other groups too: Product Owner groups, strategy groups, and occasionally members of the management cadre.

As a member of the delivery team, they have particular responsibility for "what is being delivered." The responsibility is not exclusive; other team members have views and with encouragement should share them. Still, Product Owners are first among equals when it comes to nominating what to build, and what to build next. Their skills, experience, time spent with customers (and users), research, analysis, and more mean they are (or at least should be) the best-informed people to make such decisions.

Importantly the Product Owner will need to say "No" to requests. Technology teams are usually full of good product enhancement ideas. Senior people, outside the team, will often make "suggestions" too. No team could implement every idea, and someone needs to be able to say "No."

However, every team is different and contains different skills and experience. As a result, every team will differ in what it needs from the Product Owner and how the team members can support the Product Owner and share the work. For example, the skills and focus of User Experience Designers overlap with those of Product Owners; wise Product Owners make the most of those skills. Other teams' members, especially Software Testers, bring skills and experience which can be leveraged.

Every Product Owner is themselves different and brings different skills, experience, and insights to the role, and each Product Owner has different ambitions and aim for themselves.

But a Product Owner is not some other things:

- Product Owners, who were a developer, need to accept they will not be coding anymore. There simply isn't time and, anyway, they need to trust the team.

- Product Owners who were Project Managers or Development or Line Managers should resist the urge to tell people what to do, neither should they look too far into the future. Instead they need to recognize that their authority derives from their competence not from a position in a hierarchy. They need to refocus on value not time.

- Product Owners coming from a Business Analysis background need to look beyond Business Analysis. Specifically, they need to immerse themselves in the world of Product Management.

Every Product Owner, and those working with Product Owners, needs to read and reflect on the role. There are really no hard and fast rules about what a Product Owner should or should not do.

What Are You Building?

The reoccurring question for all Product Owners is: What should be built? It occurs in sprint planning: What should be built this sprint? It occurs in thinking about the near future: What should be built next? And it occurs when thinking further out: What should be built next year? What do our future customers need?

Product ownership revolves around this question. The question is asked again and again because the world is changing—what customers bought yesterday might not be what they buy tomorrow—and because new information becomes available. Consequently, the Product Owner role, and the way they work is different from roles that came before.

Speak to any Project Manager and it isn't long before they will talk about *The Iron Triangle* or *The Triangle of Constraints*. See Figure 1-1.

© Allan Kelly 2019
A. Kelly, *The Art of Agile Product Ownership*,
https://doi.org/10.1007/978-1-4842-5168-3_1

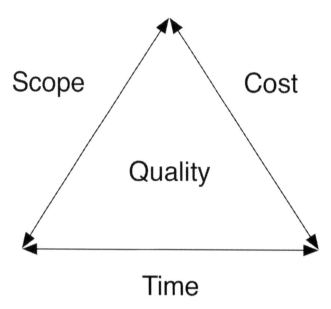

Figure 1-1. The classic iron triangle

Interestingly project success is usually measured by meeting these parameters: cost, time, and scope. But these parameters are better thought of as constraints, not success criteria. For a Product Owner, the challenge is to build a solution within these constraints. A solution which meets the scope requests and is built within the budgets of money and time.

To any given problem, there are multiple solutions. Some solutions are better than others (based on some criteria). Some of these solutions can be built within the constraints and some will exceed the constraints. Decisions on what to build need to be made within the constraints.

Put it another way: the aim is not to build the best solution possible. The aim is to build the best solution within the constraints, that is: *the best solution you can afford to build.*

Imagine you are building a railway between two major cities: Los Angeles and San Francisco, or London and Leeds, or Hong Kong and Beijing. Rather than design the best railway possible, then calculate cost and then ask for the money one starts by saying "how much can we afford?" and then asking, "what kind of railway would we get for that money?"

Cost

Since I am writing about software development, I can refine this triangle a little. Consider budget, or cost. During software development, where does the money go?

Think about that for a minute: Where does that money go? Yes, money is spent on writing code and fixing bugs, but where does the money end up? While you buy some machines, and rent time on others, on most endeavors most money is spent on people. Salaries and wage costs usually dwarf everything else.

The more people who work on the endeavor and the longer they work, the more money gets spent. Many other costs are a function of people too: office space rental, machines, software licenses, etc.

Other costs do exist, but they are insignificant in comparison. Especially now software runs in the cloud, there is less and less need to buy hardware to run the end product. So, when considering cost as a constraint, it is reasonable to talk about people instead.

Hence cost is a function of how many people need paying and how long they need to be paid for:

$$\text{Cost} = \text{People} \times \text{Time}$$

Hence the iron triangle can be refined slightly (Figure 1-2).

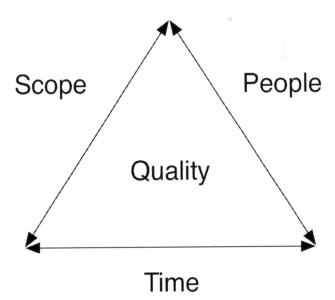

Figure 1-2. Refined iron triangle

Some commenters would go further and replace "people" with "resources" to reflect the fact that some none human resources may be needed too. I prefer not to do this because people are the heart and soul of the work. People are more than just resources and deserved to be recognized as such. I'll come back to people in a minute.

Quality

Some Project Managers try to reduce time, and therefore cost, by reducing quality. Specifically, they leave bugs unfixed and "technical debt" unpaid. Unfortunately, experience shows that such short run savings only really save money in the very very short run. Unpaid technical debt soon becomes a problem and costs increase as people battle weak code and fix bugs.

Those who have studied the economics of software development are pretty much uniform in saying that cutting quality increases costs and schedules:

> The bottom line is that poor-quality software costs more to build and to maintain than high-quality software, and it can also degrade operational performance, increase user error rates, and reduce revenue by decreasing the ability handle customer transactions or attract additional clients.

> For the software industry, not only is quality free, as stated by Phil Crosby, but it benefits the entire economic situations of both developers and clients.[1]

Therefore, let's not consider cutting quality. Quality needs to be kept high if costs and time are to be minimized.

Time

While traditional development aims for an end date, it is more often an ongoing negotiation. As projects slip, the end date is delayed—this in turn implies more costs as keeping the team staffed requires more money.

Traditional projects would postpone the end date again and again until one day it can no longer be postponed. Sooner or later—usually later—someone demands the work end.

---

[1] C. Jones, B. Bonsignour, and J. Subramanyam, *The Economics of Software Quality* (Addison-Wesley, 2011).

Agile works differently. Firstly, agile teams typically work in time boxes: two-week sprints. Every second week there is a negotiation about what will be build next.

There may be sprint followed by sprint followed by sprint, but agile teams should know how many sprints they have and when they need to be done. Provided they have a deliverable product at the end of each sprint, then meeting a final deadline is trivial. (And any team not having a shippable product at least once a fortnight really shouldn't call itself agile.)

Therefore, for an agile team, time is fixed. In the short run, the sprint creates a deadline. In the long run, the desired end date should be well known.

People

The number of people on a team is fixed in the short run simply because people cannot be added overnight. Hiring good people takes time. The best a team can hope to do is poach someone from another team in the same company.

But again, cost constraints may not allow people to be added.

And even if costs can be overcome and people can be found, there is Brooks' Law:

> Adding manpower to a late software project makes it later.[2]

Brooks' Law can be generalized as follows:

> Adding people to software development slows it down.

Therefore, on any software team, the number of people is pretty much fixed in the short run and quite possibly the long run. Of course, people can always leave the team, so team size is flexible in the other direction at any time.

Scope, requirements, "what are we building?"

So, people are fixed, costs are fixed, quality needs to be fixed at a high point, long-run deadlines have always been fixed, and short-run deadlines are fixed in agile.

---

[2] Fred Brooks, *The Mythical Man Month: Essays on Software Engineering* (Addison-Wesley, 1975).

That leaves scope. Requirements. Stories. Use case. The "thing we are building." Call it what you like—I like to call it demand. Whatever we call it, this is the only parameter which is flexible.

And someone has to make those decisions. Three guesses who that is?

My answer is The Product Owner. The Product Owner is the decision maker.

When working agile, the thing being built is in a constant state of flux both in the short term and, possibly to a lesser degree, the long term. Since the "what are we building?" question is the raison d'être for the Product Owner role, the role becomes very important.

Contrast the Project Manager

Traditional Project Managers were trained to flex everything but scope. Traditional project management saw the "what are we building" question as determined before the work begins and fixed. The job of the Project Manager is to deliver everything asked for within the constraints.

Of course, at the first sign of slippage the traditional Project Manager would ask for more time—which implies more money too.

Ignoring Brooks' Law, such Project Managers would also look to increase resources—which also increases costs. At the same time, they would lean on developers to cut quality—which would reduce quality and sap their morale and motivation.

Traditional project management held scope sacrosanct until every other option had been exhausted. (And in exhausting those other options often made the situation worse.)

If there is one difference between agile working and traditional, it is this: agile constantly flexes scope.

Hence, the Product Owner role comes to the fore and the Project Manager role steps back.

Why Have a Product Owner?

One person is responsible for managing and controlling the Product Backlog. That person is referred to as the Product Owner. ... The Product Owner is one person not a committee. ... The practice Scrum adds is that only one person is responsible for maintaining and sustaining the content and the priority of a Single Product Backlog.

—Ken Schwaber and Mike Beedle[1]

Customer: A role on the team for choosing what stories the system has to satisfy, what stories are needed first and what can be deferred, and for defining tests to verify the correct functioning of the stories.

—Kent Beck[2]

Why have a Product Owner? Even the short answer to this question comes in several parts. First, having one voice, one decision maker, increases clarity and removes conflicting requests on the delivery team.

[1] K. Schwaber and M. Beedle, *Agile Software Development with Scrum* (Addison-Wesley, 2002).
[2] Kent Beck, *Extreme Programming Explained* (Addison-Wesley, 2000).

© Allan Kelly 2019
A. Kelly, *The Art of Agile Product Ownership*,
https://doi.org/10.1007/978-1-4842-5168-3_2

The Product Owner provides a known, usually single, point of contact for those outside the team (Figure 2-1). Customers and users need someone to speak to share questions, requests, and feedback. While the team could share the role or rotate the position between them, it quickly gets confusing to those outside the team.

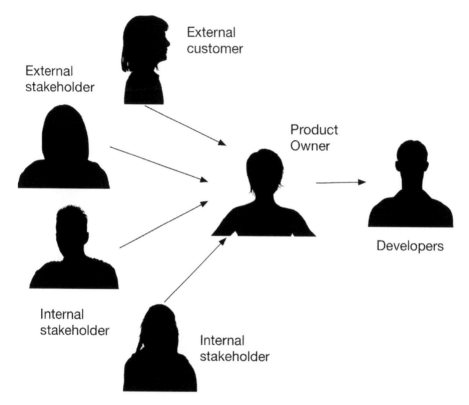

Figure 2-1. The Product Owner provides a known point of contact for those outside the team

Third, undertaking the decision maker role is a skillset in its own right. Gathering the information needed to make those decisions about stories and priorities, talking to stakeholders, managing conflicting requests, and planning for the future is itself a skillset. This skillset needs to be learned in the same way that Python and Java must be learned.

So, the question is: How many people on a team need these skills? Not everyone has such skills or the desire to learn these skills. Insisting a hard-core Haskell developer learns about stakeholder management might not your best idea. In general, it makes sense to have one person with customer facing "requirements" skills for between three and seven other team members.

The Product Owner Delta

The aim of the Product Owner is to increase, even maximize, the business value delivered by the team as a whole. The Product Owner does not so much create value themselves as increase the value created by others.

BUSINESS VALUE

Before I continue let me unpack what I mean by "business value."

By business I mean: the organization, this may be a commercial profit generating firm, a Government department or institution, a charity, an association, or any other structure which brings people together to create products, delivery services, or achieve some common goal.

By value I mean: something the organization values. Value is something of benefit. Obviously that benefit may be financial, something you can measure in dollars, pounds, euros, or any other currency. But value does not have to be monetary. Value to a hospital might be healthy patience. Value to a homeless charity might be fewer rough sleepers. Value to a Government Education department might be children reading.

In many ways "business benefit" is a better term because it is more encompassing. The software industry likes to talk about "business value," so most of the time this is the term I use.

Think of it like this: if the team randomly selected work to do and delivered it to customers, then some value would be created. (For simplicity I'll ignore the worst-case scenario where that work detracts from the existing value for the moment.) The aim of the PO is to ensure the work done creates more value than a simple random selection. The greater the difference, or delta to use a mathematical term, between random selection and an informed selection the better.

One hopes that intelligent selection of work by a skilled Product Owner will result in both more value being delivered and increasing difference between intelligent PO selected work and randomly selected work.

This difference is the value added by a Product Owner. I like to call this difference the *Product Owner Delta*—shown graphically in Figure 2-2.

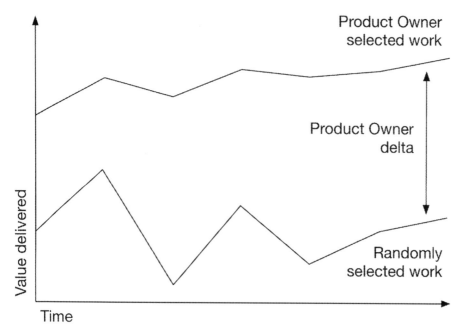

Figure 2-2. The Product Owner Delta

Now in real life work is seldom randomly so Product Owners are not competing against random selection. In some cases, the alternative to a designed Product Owners is someone else: a senior developer, an architect, some manager, or someone else. In such cases this person is taking on the Product Owner role. They may not have the title, the aptitude, the skills, or official position, but when work is selected by one person, they are de facto the Product Owner.

In other cases, the alternative to the PO might be selected by consensus on the team, or a subset of the team. Now it is entirely possible that such a group could outperform a single Product Owner in selecting such work—especially if they have market and customer knowledge, some analysis skills, time to do the work, and so on. In some cases, this works, for example, a small start-up staffed by software developers creating software development tools.

However, in some cases selection by committee might be inferior to a random selection. Imagine a team which has never met a customer, argue about what to do, duck key decisions, and never say no to any request.

There is more to increasing the Product Owner Delta than simply selecting the highest value items. Timely selection can help too. If decisions are not being made, or committees are spending a long time making decisions, then having one person simply make those decisions in an efficient, timely, manner can increase the delta.

Time has another role. Because of cost-of-delay, simply selecting the highest value items at any one point in time does not maximize the value delivered.

Single voice

Having users and customers talk directly to members of the development team can be a very effective way of working. However, it quickly becomes problematic when there are multiple customers. Even if those customers are not asking for competing work, some form of prioritization is needed, somebody has to wait, and someone needs to decide who that is.

I once managed a team of developers who were regularly interrupted by people from outside the team who wanted particular items worked on. Sales, customer service, and support staff would think nothing of walking over to a programmer's desk and saying "Could you please add feature X for customer Y." Such requests were disruptive and meant it was difficult to have a coherent approach to enhancements.

The notion of a requirements gatekeeper occurs again and again in software development methods and texts. Extreme Programming's Customer role parallels Scrum's Product Owner. Business Analysts, Product Managers, and Development Managers have often filled the same need.

Left to themselves customers and customer facing staff make many requests of the development team (Figure 2-3).

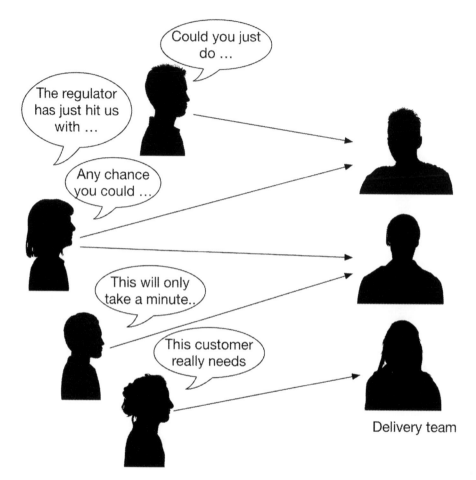

Figure 2-3. Everyone speaks directly to developers

Having a "single voice" creates clarity and forces prioritization. Many a project has been waylaid by diverse stakeholders pulling the team in different directions. Too often "decibel management" has ruled.

Using a Product Owner as a central request hub (Figure 2-4) does not mean the development team do not speak to customers. Direct contact between developers and customers is to be encouraged. Having a PO in place creates a mechanism to arbitrate between diverse requests and see them in relation to one another.

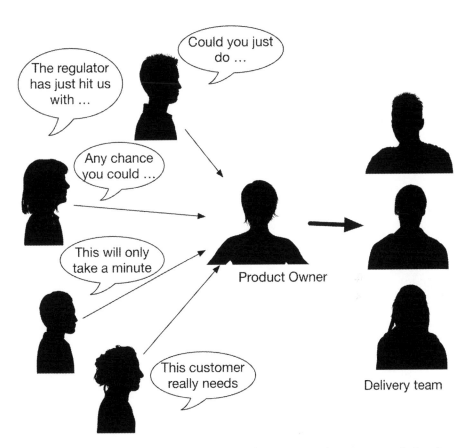

Figure 2-4. Product Owners act as a central clearing center for requests and give clear priorities to the team

Time

The Product Owner is the on-ramp for work coming into a delivery team. Not only do POs manage and prioritize the backlog to decide what gets worked on next—and after next, and next year, and so on—but they are usually the interface to the outside world. It is the PO who talks to customers and understands what customers need. It is the PO who listens to the demands of regulators and decides how to address them. And it is the PO who decides which security threats will be addressed—and which will be accepted.

While this work could be distributed around a whole team, doing so might mean the team have no time for anything else. One can always listen to one more customer or read one more security threat warning. Designating a specific individual, or individuals, to consider these issues is itself a form of time boxing which allows other team members to get on with delivery.

Designating one person allows all the information to be centralized in one head. That has some downsides, but it does mean that person has the maximum amount of information at the time the decision must be made. That also allows for one person to be answerable for the decision.

Much product discovery, customer contact, and so on happen on a different pace to development work. Customer meetings usually need to be planned in advance, sometimes months in advance. And traveling to meetings soaks up time. Someone needs to have the time to waste.

Work not to do

Actually, panning for gold is not quite the right metaphor. Perhaps more valuable than finding golden nuggets is learning which promising nuggets are fool's gold.

Every one of us has great ideas for products and new product features. So do our co-workers, customers, children, partners, ex-partners, and the woman you met at a party last week and used a competitor product 5 years ago. But every work item which is done comes at the cost of not doing something else.

Product Owners meet customers not so much to learn what to do as to learn what not to do. Finding "requirements" is the easy bit. Knowing which ones to discard is far harder. Meeting customers, attending user groups and trade shows, examining competitors, future gazing, and so on provide information to know what not to do.

Here again is a reason for separating the "what to do" decision from the "doing" work. Each of us has personal preferences over what to do, and such preferences will influence our decisions on what to do and what not to do. In particular, when work has already begun, it can be hard to cancel it. Confirmation bias means one is more likely to find supporting evidence for work that has begun, or which one would like to do.

Empathy

The best Programmers have an empathy for the code: the code speaks to them. They can feel where the code needs refactoring (redesign). They know when the code can accommodate changes and when it cannot. Even at an architectural level, technical staff work by intuitively feeling the technology— to work entirely rationally would be too time-consuming.

Similarly, Product Owners, and other customer facing staff, have empathy for actual users. They can sense the pain and frustration of someone undertaking a difficult task or working with complex software.

Sometimes code and customer empathy are in conflict: the way the program wants to work is different to the way people want to work. Having specialists in each is beneficial, one person could not fully appreciate or articulate both sides.

Tension wanted

As long as it doesn't lead to actual conflict tension can be a good thing. Having one person represent and speak for customers and another speak for the technology allows that tension to be brought into the open and addressed. Expecting one person to hold both sides of the argument in their head is asking for trouble.

People, even technology professionals, have their own biases. These biases lead them to the role they hold. Given free rein their biases may go unchecked. Having different specialists, with different biases, allows for a creative tension.

One expects the result of recognizing the differences and exposing the tension to be a better, fairer, result.

Not alone

There are good reasons to have a Product Owner, and there are good reasons why there should be one definitive voice in deciding what gets worked on next. But that does not mean the Product Owner should work alone or in isolation from the rest of the team.

The Product Owner may work with other related specialists—perhaps a Business Analyst, or a User Experience Designer, Subject Matter Expert, and others. Such specialists may even form a team-within-a-team. On other occasions, these specialists may be outside the team. It might be that the Product Owner needs to periodically call in specialist skills for short periods, but having specialists outside the team adds complications and can inject delays.

With or without other specialists, Product Owners should also harness the power of the team. Testers in particular can help Product Owners, for example, in setting acceptance criteria. To this end even the most technical team members should visit customers and take part in requirements discussions.

At the end of the day, it often comes down to skills and time. Where team members have skills to help it makes sense for them to help. When time is tight, it may be difficult to justify taking a Programmer away from the code-face to visit a customer. But if the Product Owner lacks the time to visit customers too, then it might make more sense to have the time-pressed developer talk to the customer rather than miss the opportunity to hear from a customer. If nobody has the time to validate needs with customers, then one must trust in luck.

To put it another way: during a week a team can undertake four units of work. Each unit of work adds one unit of value. If the team can now deliver a fifth unit of work, they have two options: either produce a fifth unit of value or use the fifth unit of work to better understand how those four units of work add value. Potentially, the value of each unit of work can be increased through greater understanding. Or perhaps, a more valuable piece of work can be identified.

When time is tight, it is natural to try and do more work. But it is at exactly such times that one should ask: Is the limited amount of time being used to maximum effect?

Skills

Having stated that specialist skills are a key reason for having specialist Product Owners, I have not discussed the skills required by Product Owners. Much of this book, or at least this part of the book, is concerned with those skills.

Suffice to say: there are only so many hours in a day. It is hard enough for a Programmer to keep abreast of the language and libraries of their chosen language, but mastering a full range of product ownership skills too leaves little time for sleeping. Indeed, it is doubtful if there is even enough time for a dedicated Product Owner to master all the skills they might potentially need.

Who Is the Product Owner?

The normal human reaction is to evade the priority decision by doing a little bit of everything.

—Peter Drucker[1]

At the most basic level, the Product Owner is the person who decides what gets in the next. The term originates in Scrum, but it is not unusual to find the term being used in teams following other approaches, for example, Kanban, or their own hybrid processes.

In the early descriptions of Scrum, there was a tangible feel that the Product Owner really had the authority to make decisions. They were the **owner**. I still hope that is true, but more often than not the person playing Product Owner is more likely to be a proxy for an owner or multiple real customers or stakeholders.

---

[1] Peter F. Drucker, *The Age of Discontinuity* (Elsevier, 1969).

© Allan Kelly 2019
A. Kelly, *The Art of Agile Product Ownership*,
https://doi.org/10.1007/978-1-4842-5168-3_3

There are two common problems in having a real owner, that is, a real person who wants the product, in the role. Firstly, they can lack the skills to be a Product Owner. Writing User Stories and adding them to a backlog might be easy, but that is a small part of the role. A Product Owner's other abilities need to include the following:

- Interpersonal skills to work with a team

- An understanding of technology and software development

- An appreciation of the commercial pressures to deliver products and value

- Skills to value stories and create and execute product strategy

- Focus to work in short iterations to deadline

- Ability to say No and limit work

- And more

The second problem real owners often face is time. By definition, real owners have real authority and real responsibilities. Being a Product Owner is almost a second job. Surrendering their "day job" jeopardizes authority, but keeping it can mean they lack the time to be an effective Product Owner.

PRODUCT MANAGER, PRODUCT OWNER, BUSINESS ANALYST, AND EVERYONE ELSE

It is hard to discuss the Product Owner role without referring to other roles which are also involved in the "what shall we build" question. The Product Manager and Business Analyst roles in particular need to be juxtaposed with the Product Owner.

It is entirely sensible for a Product Owner to be a trained and experienced Product Manager or Business Analyst because the three roles require very similar skillsets. In general, the title Product Owner can be considered an alias for Product Manager or Business Analyst.

Thus, I need to discuss these two roles—and some other roles such as Project Manager, Subject Matter Export, Requirements Engineer, Systems Analyst, etc. On the one hand, I should discuss these roles first so that you, the reader, understand what I am talking about. On the other hand, to discuss these roles first would get in the way of discussing the Product Owner role.

Thus, I will defer discussion of these roles. I assume the reader has some acquaintance with the other roles. A later volume will look at these roles in more depth.

Alias Product Owner

It is possible to have others fill the PO role. Provided that is, they can satisfy the four attributes: skills, authority, legitimacy, and time - chapter 5 discusses these attributes in detail. Having a qualified specialist fill the role has many advantages—especially when there are many customers.

As already noted, Scrum describes what Owners do within the Scrum setting but not how they know what they need to know to make those decisions. That knowledge comes because underneath they have real skills and experience.

For many years I have described the title Product Owner as an alias. The title Product Owner describes a specialist who, in the Scrum setting, undertakes the work defined for the Product Owner. As such the title Product Owner has often been an alias for someone who is employed in another role.

Product Owner is a Scrum defined role. In my experience the role is usually filled by a Product Manager, a BA (Business Analyst), or SME (Subject Matter Expert, sometimes called a Domain Expert) (Figure 3-1). As others have put it, "Product Owner is a role not a title." In other words: nobody should have Product Owner on their business cards.

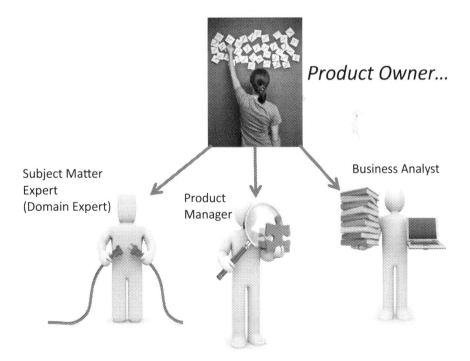

Figure 3-1. Product Owner has often been an alias which maps to Product Manager, Business Analysis, or Subject Matter Expert

While this is still true for some Product Owners, the world is no longer so clear cut. Today's Product Owners need skills from all these domains. A PO may well need product management skills, business analysis skills, and subject matter expertise.

Product Managers and Business Analysts

The Product Manager role and the Business Analyst role have a lot in common. Both roles seek an understanding of what the product needs to do and to communicate that to the team building the product. While the roles need a similar aptitude and skillset, they are different. The roles are close cousins rather than siblings.

In general Product Managers work at companies that create software that sells in a market against other products. They are outward facing. They know they need to seek out customers and find out what they need to make their lives better. Product Managers need to consider competitor products and changes outside the company.

In contrast, Business Analysts work at companies which develop software for internal use. These are specific developments for companies which are only used internally. The natural home of a BA is the corporate IT departments— and external service providers (ESP for short), "outsourcers."

Business Analysts look inward; they look at the operations and needs inside a company. They know exactly who their users are—in some cases there may only be one user. When BAs look outside the company, they may well be looking at suppliers as alternatives to development not as competitors in the market.

The similarities and differences between the Product Manager and the Business Analyst roles are often overlooked.

Project Managers?

As if the confusion between Business Analyst, Product Manager, and Product Owner were not enough, there is another role which is sometimes added to the mix: the Project Manager.

Like the Business Analyst, the Project Manager role is somewhat ill-defined and quite elastic. The standard text for the PRINCE 2 method (a popular project management technique in the United Kingdom) does not define the role of Project Manager.[2]

---

[2] Office of Government Commerce, *Tailoring PRINCE2* (London: TSO (The Stationary Office), 2002).

As a rule-of-thumb, BAs and Product Managers are concerned with the "what" of a development, while Project Managers are concerned with the "when." Beyond this different organizations slice-and-dice responsibilities differently.

While PRINCE 2 contains processes to ensure the "what" and "why" are defined (in the business case), it is silent on who should create these documents. Neither is there any guidance on how to create a business case or what skills are required to write one. This is because writing a business case is not a project manager's responsibility.

Project Managers are not Product Owners, neither are they Business Analysts or Product Managers. Project Managers have different training, different objectives, and often different experiences.

The problem

The PO as an alias for Product Manager or Business Analyst is a nice model and helps explain the world. But it has always been a model, and, as with all models, it simplifies the world to explain it. One problem with this model has always been that the different roles, Product Manager, Business Analyst, and Subject Matter Expert, have never been completely clear cut.

As business becomes increasingly digital, things are changing. As companies use more software technology, the role of software changes too. Software products are no longer an operational cost-saving mechanism. Software today is a customer facing strategic route to competitive advantage. Consequently, the roles of PO, BA, and Product Manager are evolving too.

Once upon a time, software companies sold software products. Today the same companies sell services enabled by that software. You can still buy Microsoft Word, but increasingly people use a word processing service such as Office 365 or Google Docs. The customer experience has expanded.

Once upon a time, corporations used IT to improve efficiency in operations; software technology was back office. It was there to cut costs and help fewer people deliver more. But today customers are more likely to interact with the corporation online. Consequently, the customer experience now includes a technology experience through the computer.

AIRLINES

Twenty years ago, the only people who interacted with airline systems were airline employees. I remember buying a ticket to visit the United States for the first time. I went to a travel agent, and a nice lady used a green screen to tell me what was available. Even she was not interacting with the airline systems directly. She was most likely using a GDS provided by Sabre, Galileo, or Amadeus.

Today, whether you book with Lufthansa, SouthWest, or one of the many other airlines may well come down to which has the best web site. The booking process—the system usability, clarity, speed of response—is part of the customer experience.

By focusing on stories, backlogs, and sprints, the Scrum Product Owner role simplified the "what shall we build?" question. Scrum was good because it highlighted the need for a Product Owner. But at the same time, by simplifying the role, it overlooked important skills. Product Owner roles were a pale shadow of the Product Manager role, and the Business Analysis aspects often overlooked.

Today Business Analysts need to be able to think like Product Managers, and Product Managers need to be able to think like Business Analysts. A new variant of the BA has appeared in the job market reflecting these changes: the Digital Business Analyst.

There is still some validity to those who proclaim "Product Managers are not Product Owners" or "Business Analysts are not Product Owners," but the world has advanced and got messier. The world needs a new model.

Modern Product Owner model

The employment market has decided: *Product Owner is the role*. The Product Owner role deals with the demand side, requirements, and discovery. This is the role which considers needs and decides what gets built.

The collision between the world of Business Analysts and Product Managers is now complete. The Product Owner is now a superset of Product Manager and Business Analyst. See Figure 3-2.

Figure 3-2. Product Owner is now a superset of Product Manger, Business Analyst, and Subject Matter Expert

A Product Owner today may find they need to play the role of Business Analyst, Product Manager, and Subject Matter Expert. Product Owners today may well need the skills of business analysis. They are even more likely to need the skills of product management. And they will need to know about the domain. However you look at it, Product Owners need a wide variety of skills (Figure 3-3).

Today's Product Owner may well come from a Subject Matter Expert background. In such cases they need to learn about product ownership, Product Management, and Business Analysis.

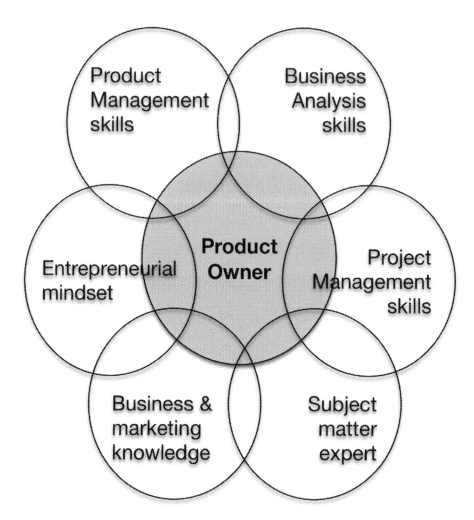

Figure 3-3. Product Owners' skillsets

Or they may have a business analysis background and need to absorb Product Management skills. Those who come from a product management background will need to learn some business analysis. In either case they will learn about the domain, but they may want to bring in a subject matter expert too.

To make things harder, exactly which skills they need, and which skills are most important, is going to vary from team to team and position to position.

Mixing roles

The modern Product Owner role is one of understanding what will make a product or service competitive in the marketplace. As such most of the role will closely resemble the Product Manager role. They will need to look outside the company to decide "what the right thing to build" is.

The modern Product Owner needs to be part Business Analyst. They need to consider how the product serves the company and how the company works with the product.

Some Product Owners will find they are primarily looking inside the organization in order to improve the organization, and the services they deliver using technology. They will need to examine internal process and talk to internal stakeholders. Using business analysis skills, they will determine "the right thing to build" and communicate it to the team.

Increasingly roles overlap and the lines between them blur. Every Product Owner needs to consider where they lie on this spectrum from internal to external, from BA to Product Manager (Figure 3-4).

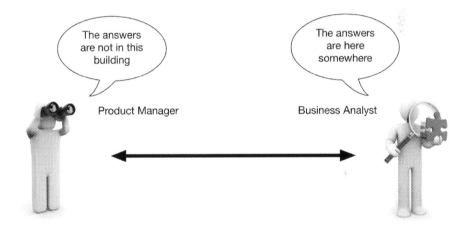

Figure 3-4. Product Owners need to determine where they fall between Product Management and Business Analysis

Product Owners will need other skills too: domain expertise, leadership, and even technical skills. Every Product Owner needs to decide for themselves what their role calls for. They should ask themselves: What are the skills I need? And how can I best help this team and this organization?

Requirements, Discovery, and Demand

The picture of the software designer deriving his design in a rational, error-free way from a statement of requirements is quite unrealistic. No system has ever been built that way, and probably none ever will. Even the small program developments shown in textbooks and papers are unreal. They have been revised and polished until the author has shown us what he wishes he had done, not what actually did happen.

—David L. Parnas and Paul C. Clements[1]

Product Owners, Business Analysts, and Product Managers are primarily concerned with the "what shall we build?" question. They may be considering this in the short term "what shall we build this sprint?" or the long term "what shall we build in five years?"

---

[1] D. L. Parnas and P. C. Clements, "A Rational Design Process: How and Why to Fake It," *IEEE Transactions on Software Engineering* 12, no. 2 (1986): 251–57; D. L. Parnas and P. C. Clements, "A Rational Design Process: How and Why to Fake It," in *Software Fundamentals: Collected Papers of David L. Parnas*, ed. D. M. and Weiss Hoffman (Addison-Wesley, 2001).

© Allan Kelly 2019
A. Kelly, *The Art of Agile Product Ownership*,
https://doi.org/10.1007/978-1-4842-5168-3_4

Traditionally software development answered such questions with *Requirements*. *The Requirements* described—in writing—what needed building. Embodied in this concept was the assumptions that the thing to be built could be defined and that defining the thing would be beneficial.

The rise and fall of requirements

In the classical model, a requirements phase would precede development of the software product. Only once the requirements—and specifications—had been pinned down would development officially commence.

The term *specification* is colloquially used as a synonym for requirements. Strictly speaking the terms mean different things. A specification is a constrained form of a requirement. A requirement describes the desired result, while a specification is far more, well, specific.

Under the classical model, software developers believed that provided requirements (and specifications) could be detailed and accurate enough, then most—if not all—problems would be solved. Naturally, once decided requirements and specification should not be changed—they were "frozen."

In the extreme this led to the creation of formal mathematical proofs. At University I learned to write these detailed requirements and specifications using formal logic. While exact these requirements were unintelligible to most people—even experienced Programmers - Such "specifications" were little different from program code.

For multiple reasons—not least the rise of agile software development—the assumptions underlying the notion of requirements have been challenged.

To start with the idea of written requirements came into question. Some pointed out that the written word is not a great way to share knowledge. Others pointed out that large requirements documents take time to write, cost money to write, and seldom get read in depth. When they do get read, the reader seldom remembers much.

Software metrics expert Capers Jones has some interesting observations on requirements documents:

> the widely used concept that quality means "conformance to require-ments" is illogical as a serious quality definition. Requirements errors themselves constitute one of the major problem areas of the software industry (about 15 percent of defect totals).[2]

---

[2] C. Jones, *Applied Software Measurement* (McGraw Hill, 2008).

Requirements documents form a significant proportion of all system documentation:

> What is astonishing about paperwork volumes for very large systems is that the specifications and technical documents can be large enough to go beyond the normal lifetime reading speed of a single analyst![3]

Assume for a moment that one could write down requirements in sufficient detail, free of errors, and communicate them perfectly to the development team. There is still a bigger problem.

Traditionally requirements determination was separated from development which was separated from deployment and usage (Figure 4-1). It could be impossible, or very difficult, to incorporate feedback from user experience.

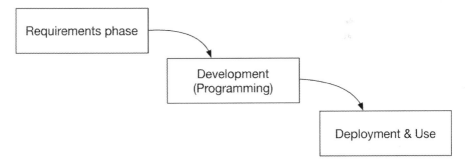

Figure 4-1. The traditional "waterfall" development paradigm

The world changes.

Commercial needs drive most software creation. While software development is happening, the commercial world continues to change and evolve. Much of this change is because technology itself evolves and changes. New technologies create new opportunities.

Some teams still try to pin requirements down before they start working. Some teams still resist changes to requirements once work has begun. Some people still believe defined, fixed, requirements are an essential foundation for successful software. If it works, then fine, these people are free to continue, but many teams have abandoned this approach as they adopt agile.

The basis of agile software development is the belief that it is better for a team to be flexible and responsive to changing requirements rather than highly adapted to fixed requirements.

---

[3] Ibid.

When this starting assumption is wrong, the effects are very different:

- If a team assumes requirements are known and will not change, then any changes will create significant problems.

- If a team assumes requirements are vague and will change then if requirements do not change, they will still succeed.

As a result, the agile approach is valid whether the assumption (of stable requirements) is right or wrong. If requirements change, then the assumption holds and the team works with changing requirements. If the requirements don't change, then the team still delivers. Conversely, if the assumption of fixed requirements is wrong, then the team encounters problems.

Discovery

As a result of the rise of agile software development, teams take a more flexible approach to requirements. Teams assume the need is vague, they assume requirements will emerge as work progresses, and they assume that value will become visible during the work.

Rather than talk about requirements—which are assumed to be known—they prefer to talk about discovery.

The aim of the team is to discover the customer needs and discover the value of those needs. A little discovery may occur before any code gets written, but importantly discovery will continue during product development.

The discovery model (Figure 4-2) assumes rapid feedback both from users of the product and from the market reaction to the product. Feedback from the development team is incorporated even before customers see the product.

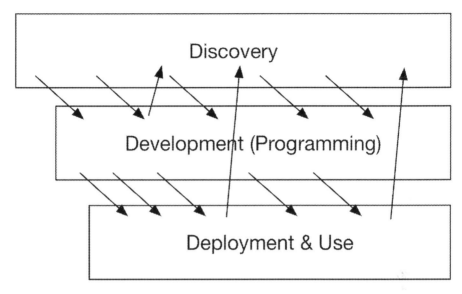

Figure 4-2. Requirements discovery, development, deployment, and use are all happening in parallel

Discovery may start before doing, but the model assumes overlapping activities feeding back to one another.

Some have referred to this model as Dual-Track: a discovery track and a development track operating in parallel (Jeff Patton[4] and Marty Cagan[5] may have been the originators of "dual-track" and have both written about it). Requests from the discovery track to the delivery track may still be called "requirements," but the term is vestigial and does not come with the assumptions of perfect foresight.

The demand side

The question "what shall we build?" is non-trivial. I like to apply economic thinking here: there is supply and demand (Figure 4-3).

---

[4] Jeff Patton, "Dual Track Development Is Not Duel Track," *Dual Track Development Is Not Duel Track* (blog), https://jpattonassociates.com/dual-track-development/.
[5] Cagan, *Inspired: How to Create Products Customers Love* (SVPG Press, 2008).

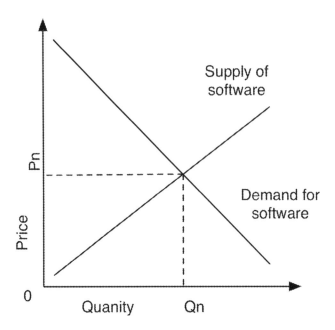

Figure 4-3. Software development can be thought about using economists supply and demand models

The supply side is easy: software supply is the activity of building and delivering software. It is programming, design, development, engineering; it is operations, DevOps, and so on. Most of the thinking around agile software development discusses software supply—and increasing software supply at that.

The demand side is somewhat more complex. In part this is because assumptions around supply model influence how requests are presented. And in part this is because much demand for software does not exist—or at least is not visible—until one understands what technology can do.

Who needed e-mail until they saw e-mail? Who knew they needed e-mail connectivity 24x7 in their pocket until they saw an iPhone?

The history of "texting"—the Short Message System (SMS) to give it the correct name—is illuminating here. SMS was originally devised as technical capability for the engineers designing GSM phone systems. No customer asked for SMS. Nobody requested a 160-character messaging system in their pocket.

Even after SMS texting exploded in Europe in the early 2000s, American telcos failed to market SMS or opened gateways between their networks. A PacBell subscriber could not text an AT&T subscriber. For some years the Americans didn't feel any need for something which had become essential in Europe.

Today cellphone users in the United States alone send over six billion messages a day.

Changing requirements to discovery

As upfront requirements documents have given way to dynamic dual-track product discovery, the nature of the work has changed. At the turn of the millennium, it was common to find Product Managers writing BRDs (Business Requirements Documents) which begat MRDs (Market Requirements Document). Development teams would take the MRD and may create an FRD (Features Requirements Document.)

Business Analysts followed a similar process with different document names. A Business Case would begat a Functional Spec which might begat a Program Spec.

The emphasis was on upfront definition. To do this Product Managers and Business Analysts would extensively research and analyze the need, the problem, the opportunity. They would conduct user interviews, examine market trends and similar systems; they would run focus groups and requirements workshops.

These models were born in the late 1960s and early 1970s. Even though the models evolved, they still embodied the assumption that programming was expensive and slow. That was true in the 1970s because computers did have limited in resources.

In the 1970s it made sense to do upfront analysis and documentation because CPU cycles were expensive relative to paper. The machines were limited resources, so moving activities away from machines was more efficient.

Now, computers are an order of magnitude more powerful. Today it can be far faster, and cheaper, to program something—perhaps using quick prototyping and wire framing tools—put it in front of customers and see what the reaction is. Today's programming tools make it far easier to discover needs by building something and observing the result. Testing in the market allows rapid analysis of commercial opportunities with real data.

One could argue that agile software development has driven this trend. Agile lends itself to this style of working because teams work in short iterations to produce small product increments while responding to changing needs rather than adhering to plan.

But this confuses cause and effect. Agile is itself the result of the increases in CPU power. Massively more powerful machines have reduced the time and cost of creating viable products which can provide useful feedback.

Agile is a process which allows utilization of cheap ubiquitous CPU cycles. When the relative prices changed, the economics changed. Sticking with the traditional process would not utilize the cheap CPU cycles. Cheap CPU cycles make a more efficient process possible.

Today, CPU cycles are cheap. Therefore, in relative terms, upfront activities—analysts and documentation—are expensive. Far better to exploit cheap CPU cycles.

The move from requirements to discovery is simply economics.

Role changes

For product specialists (Product Owners, Product Managers, and Business Analysts), these changes mean their roles need to change too. Detailed research and analysis, captured in a document, gives way to experimentation, face-to-face conversations, analysis of results, feedback, and iteration.

Those on the demand side can still learn from research reports. They can—and should—still interview users and customers about their needs. Performing stakeholder analysis, observing customers, and holding focus groups can still produce useful insights. And I still recommend all product specialists read *The Economist* to keep abreast of global and commercial changes.

But while these activities once constituted the bulk of the product specialist work, they are now a small part. The learning offered by these activities is still valuable, but, in market experiments offer rapid learning which is even more valuable.

Analysis today is more likely than not to be undertaken after customers see a product than before. Product specialists should now be working with teams to create products, then observing and analyzing the results. Technology can help here too: the likes of Google Analytics and screen recording systems can provide data for analysis

Instead of creating defined requirements product specialists may create hypothesis and experiments. They create a small piece of product and oversee how customers react. Analyzing the result determines the next action: refine the experiment, expand the experiment, or forget about it and try something different.

Sometimes this process gets called *Build-Measure-Learn*. Although this is itself a variation on the Shewhart cycle: Plan-Do-Check-Act.

There is nothing wrong with upfront planning and analysis. However, it has rapidly diminishing returns. The first five minutes offer fantastic returns on investment. But after two hours of planning, another five minutes will make little difference. And after four hours, each extra minute probably has a negative return on investment (ROI).

Do a little planning. Then build something. See what happens. Analyze the result. Learning is rapid in these stages and the return on time spent is high. Now repeat.

Every Product Owner Needs Four Things

I sincerely believe there are better Product Owners and not-so-good Product Owners. There are some organizations (teams, companies, enterprises) which offer a better environment for product ownership, and equally there are those which are downright hostile to product ownership.

To be an effective Product Owner, one needs at least four things.

Skills and experience

There is more to being a Product Owner than simply writing user stories and prioritizing a backlog. Yes, you need to know how to work with a development team and how to work in an agile-style process. Yes, you need to be able to write user stories and acceptance criteria. Perhaps BDD (Behavior Driven Development) style "Cucumber" acceptance criteria too. Yes, you need to be able to manage a backlog and prioritize and partake in planning meetings.

But how do you know what should be a priority?

© Allan Kelly 2019
A. Kelly, *The Art of Agile Product Ownership*,
https://doi.org/10.1007/978-1-4842-5168-3_5

How do you know what will deliver value? What will please customers? Satisfy stakeholders?

Importantly Product Owners need to be able to do the work behind the backlog. Prioritizing and refining backlogs does not happen in isolation. To work effectively, POs need a constant flow of current information.

Any idiot can pick random items from a backlog, but it takes skills and experience to maximize value. Product Owners need to meet people, hold conversations, and think about what they have learned. If necessary, they need to do analysis and revisit the conversation to dig deeper.

Product Owners need to be able to identify users, segment customers, interview people, and understand their needs and jobs to be done. They need to know when to run experiments and when to turn to research journals and market studies. And that might mean they need data analysis skills too.

If the product is going to sell as a commercial product, you will need wider product management skills. Those creating products for internal use will find business analysis skills vital.

As a PO you may also need specialist domain knowledge—you might need to be a subject matter expert in your own right; or you might become an SME yourself given time.

Some understanding of business strategy, finance, marketing, process analysis and design, user experience design, and more.

Don't underestimate the skills and experience you need to be an effective Product Owner.

Authority

At the very least, a Product Owner needs the authority to nominate the work the team will do during the next two weeks. They need the authority to choose items from a backlog and ask the team to do them. They need the authority not to have their decisions overridden on a regular basis. (OK, it happens occasionally.)

As a general rule, the more authority the Product Owner has, the more effective they are going to be in their role.

The organization may confer that authority, but the team need to recognize and accept it too.

I've seen many Product Owners who while they have the authority to nominate work for a team don't have the authority to throw things out of the backlog. When the only way for a story to leave the backlog is for it to get developed, things get very expensive. This leads to constipated backlogs stuffed full of worthless rubbish and where one can't see the wood for the trees.

If the Product Owner doesn't have sufficient authority, then either they need to borrow some or there is going to be trouble.

Legitimacy

Legitimacy is different from authority. Legitimacy means one is recognized as the right person, the bonafide person to exercise authority and do the background work to find out what they need to find out in order to make those decisions.

Legitimacy means the Product Owner can go and meet customers if they want. And it means that they will get their expenses paid.

Legitimacy means that nobody else is trying to fill the Product Owner role or undermine them. In particular it means the team respect the Product Owner and trust them to make the right calls. Most of all they accept that once in a while—hopefully not too often—the Product Owner will say: "I accept technologically X is the right thing but commercially it must be Y; full ahead and damn the torpedoes."

It can be hard for a Product Owner to fill their role if the team believe someone else should be managing the backlog and prioritizing work to do. That doesn't mean the Product Owner should freeze out willing helpers; if a developer—or anyone else—takes an interest in customers and prioritization, then the PO should seek to enlist their help. But balance is required, and the first step may be to simply acknowledge someone is interested in helping.

Executives, managers, and especially sales teams need to recognize the PO as legitimate. In many organizations the question of "what should be built next" has in the past been left to development and other managers. Managers accustomed to having such authority need to accept the PO as legitimate and not override their decisions.

Similarly, sales staff need to recognize the legitimacy of the Product Owner too. Sales people can become accustomed to using the promise of a big sale to direct development to their own priorities. Product Owners will sometimes need to tell a sales person that a feature they claim is essential to a client will not get delivered soon—or perhaps at all.

Time

Finally, and probably the most difficult: Product Owners need time to do their work.

They need time to meet customers and reflect on those encounters.

They need time to work the backlog, value stories, weed out expired or valueless stories, think about the product vision, talk to stakeholders and more senior people, and then ponder what happens next.

Time to evaluate what has been delivered and see if it is delivering the expected value. Time to understand whether delivered enhancements generate more or less value than expected. Time to feedback those findings into future work, then recalibrate expected values and priorities, generate more work, or invalidate other work.

Product Owners need time to look at competitor products and consider alternatives—if only to steal ideas!

They need time to work with the technical team: have conversations about stories, expand on acceptance criteria, review work in progress, perhaps test completed features, and socialize with the team.

Much of this work requires more than just time, it requires time at the right time. Deferring a conversation because of time pressure may mean that important information is unknown at the right time. Failure to work with the team at the right time might mean work needs repeating or fails to deliver the potential value.

They also need time to enhance their own skills and learn more about the domain.

And if they don't have the time to do this?

Without time they will rush into planning meetings saying "I've been so busy, I haven't looked at the backlog this week, just bear with me while I choose some stories…."

More often than not, they will wing it and substitute opinion and guesswork instead of solid analysis, facts, and data. They overlook competition and fail to listen to the team and other managers.

And O yes, they need time for their own lives and family.

Superhuman

I sometimes think that only superhumans need apply for a Product Owner role, or perhaps many Product Owners are set up to fail from day 1. Yet the role is so important.

In one of the earliest studies of the XP Customer role—which parallels the Scrum Product Owner role—Angela Martin[1] found: "the customers [role] had the most pressured and stressful role in the project, requiring significantly more effort than the development team members."

In part Martin suggested this was because: "it is far too easy for anything that is not to do with programming, or that is not explicit covered by XP's practices, to be defined as a 'business' requirement, and thus, to become the sole responsibility of the customer."

---

[1] A. Martin, R. Biddle, and J. Noble, "The XP Customer Role in Practice: Three Studies," 2004.

Customers, Users, and Stakeholders

There is only one valid definition of a business purpose: to create a customer.

—Peter Drucker[1]

Personally, I dislike the term "user" because it does not respect those who engage with products, rather it makes those who use computer products sound like drug addicts. That said, "user" is the term the IT industry has adopted. No other term is as widely known.

The term customer is a potential alternative to user and does command respect. However, I think the two terms are used to describe different types of people.

---

[1] Peter F. Drucker, *The Practice of Management* (Harper & Row, 1954).

© Allan Kelly 2019
A. Kelly, *The Art of Agile Product Ownership*,
https://doi.org/10.1007/978-1-4842-5168-3_6

Both customers and users—whether the terms describe the same people or different people—are both examples of stakeholders. But there are potentially far more stakeholders of any product, system, or service than there are customers, or users.

Because Product Managers traditionally focus on products for use outside the company, they tend to think about customers—some of whom may be users. In contrast Business Analysts tend to consider stakeholders—who may or may not be users.

Customer or user?

The Oxford English Dictionary defines *customer* as: "a person who buys goods or services from a shop or business." The same dictionary defines *user* as "a person who uses or operates something." There is a commercial aspect to customer which users lack.

When one considers a company like Facebook, this becomes important. Facebook (currently) has over one billion users, but few of these are customers, few of them pay any money. Facebook customers, the source of revenues, number a few thousand or tens of thousands.

A colloquial definition states "You have a customer's credit card number, users don't pay." This certainly passes the Facebook test.

While important the commercial aspect is not the only thing that marks a customer as different from a user. My own definition of a customer has been: "A customer has choice, they can choose to use your product, use an alternative, or even use nothing."

My definition fails the Facebook test but highlights how users are often captive and have little choice but to use the software they are given to use.

Stakeholders

> *Requirements ultimately begin and end with people—stakeholders.*
>
> —Alexander and Beus-Dukic[2]

---

[2] I. Alexander and L. Beus-Dukic, *Discovering Requirements* (Chichester: John Wiley & Sons, 2009).

> *A stakeholder is a person group or object, which has some direct or indirect interest in a system. Stakeholder can exercise control over both the immediate system operational characteristics, as well as over long-term system lifecycle considerations.*
>
> —Tom Gilb[3]

The first challenge facing a Business Analyst is normally stakeholder identification: Who are the stakeholders? The second challenge is to understand their stake: Why do they have an interest? Is their interest legitimate? Are they active or passive in holding their stake?

Traditional business analysis has positioned stakeholder identification as an upfront activity which is done in the early phases of work. In an agile setting, it might be better seen as an ongoing exercise as new stakeholders become involved and others step back.

The third challenge with stakeholder is to keep them involved; at the most basic level, this means communicating progress to them—and perhaps delivering bad news. Again, in an agile setting, ongoing stakeholder management will involve far more: demonstrating evolving software to stakeholders, receiving their feedback, listening to their new ideas, evaluating new requests, and, perhaps most importantly, evaluating the impact and value changes are having as they are delivered.

It is important to recognize that all stakeholders are not equal. Some will have more influence than others, some will think they (should) have more influence, some will be able to articulate their need, and others will find it hard to see how technology impacts them. Most of all though, stakeholders will not have consistent views or demands:

> *Stakeholders often have different views on what is important about a business system and the improvements that are needed. These views are often contradictory and can lead to hidden agenda, conflicts and inconsistent priorities.*
>
> —Debra Paul and Donald Yeats[4]

Different but overlapping

All customers are stakeholders (Figure 6-1). All users are stakeholders too. But not all users are customers—some users have no choice but to use the product.

---

[3] T. Gilb, *Competitive Engineering* (Butterworth-Heinemann, 2005).
[4] Debra Paul and Donald Yates, eds., *Business Analysis* (The British Computer Society, 2006).

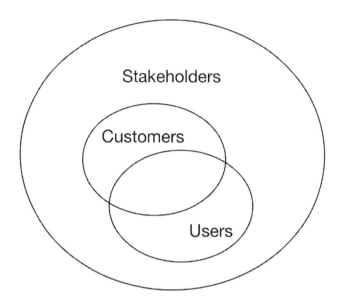

Figure 6-1. Stakeholders, customers, and users

And not all customers will use the product—think of the CFO who agrees a purchase but never uses the product.

For example, much of this book has been written on an Apple Mac computer. This makes me an Apple user and by implication an Apple stakeholder. Since I chose and paid for the Mac, I am also an Apple customer. In contrast, if I had written this book on a Dell laptop supplied by an employer, then I would be a Dell user, and stakeholder, but not a Dell customer. In that case someone else, perhaps the head of IT, would be the Dell customer (and stakeholder). They may also be a Dell user, or they may use another brand of PC.

In many ways it is the stakeholders who are neither customers nor users who are the most interesting—although not necessarily the most important. Such stakeholders get overlooked if analysis only considers customers and/or users. But it is precisely because such stakeholders are unusual that they deserve attention.

What Product Owners Do?

Product Owners are primarily concerned with the "what." They have specialist skills in determining what should be build. Any authority they hold comes from the recognition that they have such skills and are the legitimate person to decide what should be built.

As such almost all their work revolves around deciding what should be built, helping get that built, and validating that the thing that was built satisfies the original need they set out to meet.

In this part of the book, I'd like to turn my attention to what Product Owners actually do all day long. In my experience, most people answer this question with a long list of things like "write user stories" and "refine the backlog." That is but the tip of the iceberg (Figure 1).

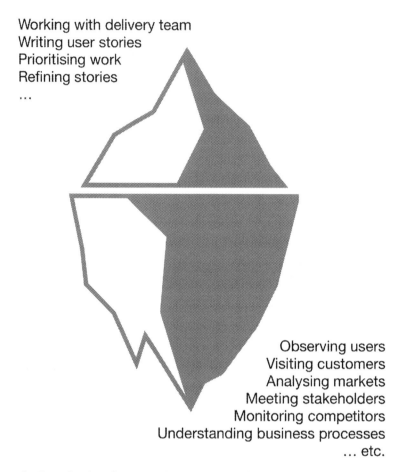

Working with delivery team
Writing user stories
Prioritising work
Refining stories
…

Observing users
Visiting customers
Analysing markets
Meeting stakeholders
Monitoring competitors
Understanding business processes
… etc.

Figure I. Some Product Owner work is very visible; far more is less visible and too easily overlooked

Yes, Product Owners write user stories. Yes, Product Owners refine the backlog. Yes, Product Owners prioritize stories, work with the delivery team, set acceptance criteria, and an awful lot more. One of the upcoming chapters talks about all that stuff.

But… you have to ask yourself:

- How does the Product Owner know what to write user stories about?

- How does the Product Owner know the things that allow them to refine the backlog?

- Where does a Product Owner get the specialize knowledge that allows them to prioritize the backlog?

There is more to the Product Owner role than stories, backlogs, and so on. There is an awful lot of iceberg which isn't seen, work which the Product Owner needs to do in order to be able to do all those things that usually get talked about.

If you will allow me to change metaphors, I sometimes likened the work of the Product Owner to that of an actor. Every one of us can see the work of the actor when they are on stage. But in order to walk on stage and play their part, there is a lot of preparation.

You don't see the actor waiting in the wings watching for the moment they will come on stage.

You don't see the actor before the performance, dressing in their costume, putting on makeup, and perhaps double checking their lines.

Nor do you see the actor in learning their lines and rehearsing, again and again before the first night. There is so much more to acting in a play than the actual performance in front of the audience. And the same is true for the Product Owner. The onstage work of actors and Product Owners is the tip of the iceberg. There is a lot more of offstage work—the iceberg below the water.

When onstage in the team, the Product Owner is seen writing user stories, prioritizing the backlogs, and such. In order to do that work effectively, there is much offstage work: visiting customers, observing or gently questioning the customers, analyzing competitor offerings, taking the views of disparate stakeholders, reading market analysis, looking at market growth forecasts, and more.

Product Owners needs to engage in all this offstage work so that their work on stage is valuable and does not misdirect the team.

In the next few chapters, I will look at what the Product Owner does on stage and some of the things they should be doing offstage in preparation. I will also look at what Product Owners should not be doing

Scrum and the Product Owner

Innovation has nothing to do with how many R&D dollars you have. When Apple came up with the Mac, IBM was spending at least 100 times more on R&D. It's not about money. It's about the people you have, how you're led, and how much you get it.

—Steve Jobs[1]

The title *Product Owner* comes from Scrum, so it makes sense to go to the source, the latest (2017) Scrum Guide:

The Product Owner is responsible for maximizing the value of the product resulting from work of the Development Team. How this is done may vary widely across organizations, Scrum Teams, and individuals.

---

[1] David Kirkpatrick, "The Second Coming of Apple Through a magical fusion of man—Steve Jobs—and company, Apple is becoming itself again: the little anticompany that could," *Fortune*, November 9, 1998.

© Allan Kelly 2019
A. Kelly, *The Art of Agile Product Ownership*,
https://doi.org/10.1007/978-1-4842-5168-3_7

The Product Owner is the sole person responsible for managing the Product Backlog. Product Backlog management includes:

- Clearly expressing Product Backlog items;

- Ordering the items in the Product Backlog to best achieve goals and missions;

- Optimizing the value of the work the Development Team performs;

- Ensuring that the Product Backlog is visible, transparent, and clear to all, and shows what the Scrum Team will work on next; and,

- Ensuring the Development Team understands items in the Product Backlog to the level needed.

The Product Owner may do the above work or have the Development Team do it. However, the Product Owner remains accountable. The Product Owner is one person, not a committee.

The Product Owner may represent the desires of a committee in the Product Backlog, but those wanting to change a Product Backlog item's priority must address the Product Owner. For the Product Owner to succeed, the entire organization must respect his or her decisions. The Product Owner's decisions are visible in the content and ordering of the Product Backlog. No one is allowed to tell the Development Team to work from a different set of requirements, and the Development Team isn't allowed to act on what anyone else says. [2]

In addition, the Scrum Guide clearly states the Product Owner is a member of the delivery team:

The Scrum Team consists of a Product Owner, the Development Team, and a Scrum Master. Scrum Teams are self-organizing and cross-functional.

The Scrum guide is mostly silent on how the Product Owner fills this role, and as such the role is open to massive interpretation. While this has the advantage of both keeping the description short and allowing variations as needed, it still leaves open the question how the Product Owner knows what they need to know to do these things.

---

[2] Ken Schwaber and Jeff Sutherland, "The Scrum Guide: The Definitive Guide to Scrum" (2017), www.scrumguides.org/download.html.

For example, in order for the Product Owner to optimize the value of the work, they need to understand the value of each item. Unless this comes from an external source, the Product Owner needs skills to determine value. They also need to understand cost of delay, the competitive pressures in the market, and longer-term strategy.

If the PO is simply presented with this information from an external source, then they are little more than a backlog administrator, and they, indeed the whole team, lack autonomy and the motivation that comes from controlling one's own work.

It is clear therefore that Product Owners need skills above and beyond those described in the Scrum Guide—and taught on most Scrum training courses. In order to understand both what the Product Owner does and what skills, they need then examining related roles will shed some light. The following chapters will do just this.

Product Owner vs. Scrum Master

It annoys me that Scrum Master get so much more attention in the software industry than the Product Owner role. This might be because the Scrum Master role has a more exciting title, it might be because Scrum Master certification has become the gateway qualification for working on an agile team, or it might be because the Product Owner role is so often misunderstood.

Whatever the reason it seems to me that a lot more is written about the Scrum Master role and how to work as a Scrum Master. Less attention is paid to the Product Owner role, but to my mind the role is so much more important.

If a Scrum Master performs badly, the team simply fails to perform well. If the Product Owner performs badly, the whole product is in jeopardy.

Scrum Masters are fond of saying "My aim is to do myself out of a job." The Scrum Master role is nominally a temporary role; once a team reaches a self-organizing state, they don't need their help anymore.

It is hard to imagine that ever being true of the Product Owner role. Teams which dispense with the Product Owner are quite likely to lose their understanding of business value and lose focus on customers.

The Scrum Master role can be—and often is—adequately filled on a part time basis on a team. A team with a part-time Product Owner may look busy, but the value they deliver will be below that they could deliver.

Onstage Product Owner

True ignorance is not the absence of knowledge, but the refusal to acquire it.

—Karl Popper, Philosopher (1902–1994)

As you read this list of things the Product Owner should be doing as part of the team to keep the agile/scrum process working effectively, ask yourself:

> What knowledge does the Product Owner need in order to do this effectively?

Writing user stories

If I had asked you to write a list of the things you think a Product Owner should do, I am sure most readers would have written down "writing user stories" first.

True, most Product Owners will write plenty of User Stories. But...

The thing normally called a "User Story" is more correctly called a *product backlog item* or simply a *story*. It is a token for work to be done.

© Allan Kelly 2019
A. Kelly, *The Art of Agile Product Ownership*,
https://doi.org/10.1007/978-1-4842-5168-3_8

"User Story" is actually a description of the format: "As a ... I want ... So that ...." Product Owners are free to use whatever format they like—free text, Use Case, Given When Then, IEEE 830, or whatever they find works best. That said, User Story format has two great features.

First, it provides Who, What, Why—who wants this thing, what do they want, and why do they want it.

Second, user stories are simple and easy for the uninitiated to understand. Techniques such as Use Cases are in many ways better at analyzing user need and precisely capturing the need. But Use Cases form a barrier between experts—who are well versed in the technique—and the lay user who does not appreciate the subtleties of the approach.

Whatever format is used, one can expect a Product Owner to spend a lot of time creating and working with such work items.

But there is no reason why a Product Owner should be the only person allowed to write user stories. Indeed, other team members can help a busy Product Owner, and other team members have insights and see opportunities which may well be captured in user stories.

Nor is it just team members who may write stories. Other stakeholders may suggest, or request, stories. In fact, stories can come from just about anyone, including the final customer.

Administering the backlog

In all likelihood the Product Owner is the backlog administrator. Indeed, too many Product Owners struggle to have the authority and legitimacy to be much more than a backlog administrator.

At its most basic level, the Product Owner is the backlog gatekeeper. They get to decide what should be added to the backlog and what should not.

More importantly the Product Owners should get to decide what is taken out of the backlog, that is, what should **not** be developed into product.

Prioritizer in chief

Continuing on from backlog administration—but requiring a little more authority—the Product Owner is the one who gets to decide what priority is attached to backlog items. In particular, it is the Product Owner who decides what will be worked on next.

For Scrum and XP teams, this means the Product Owner gets to decide in the planning meetings what items will be loaded into the sprint for the next iteration. On Kanban teams this means the Product Owner decides what is scheduled next when a slot becomes available.

Many Product Owner will find it useful to keep their backlog in some kind of priority order most of the time. This will simplify their own work—because they know what needs the most attention—and serves as a form of communication with stakeholders.

However, holding rigid priorities, prioritizing into the far future (e.g., more than 12 weeks out), and not being prepared to fast-track new valuable work are all behaviors which will cause problems. Such behaviors while appearing to offer certainty and predictability will reduce agility.

Working with the team

It shouldn't need saying but the Product Owner is there to help the team and as such much of their work will involve working with the team. Again, the Product Owner is the specialist in understanding what is needed; therefore, they need to communicate their understanding to the team.

This communication isn't a single event, it is an ongoing series of exchanges. Consider a user story, it is often said that a user story is a placeholder for a conversation. More likely or not, that conversation is between a developer and a Product Owner. It is great when a developer can talk to a user/customer directly; potentially the Product Owner need not be part of the conversation, but they may want to be part of it anyway.

Nor is that conversation a single event either. The conversation is an ongoing dialogue which starts with the story and is only finished when the story is done and accepted. (Even then the conversation may continue via another story.)

Some of that conversation will occur during the refinement and planning meeting, or in a "3-Amigos" sessions.

At any point during development, a Developer—or a Tester—may have reason to reopen the conversation and ask questions. It is impossible to know in advance every detail that will be involved even on simple changes.

Refining stories

As part of their administration duties, Product Owners will regularly review the items in the backlog and change them. This is a process called refinement.[1]

---

[1] In some circles this exercise has been called *grooming*. However, in England, this term has taken on negative connotations with the general public in recent years and is better avoided.

During refinement the words on a story may be tweaked to make it clearer, the story might be dropped or deprioritized, acceptance criteria may be enhanced, the story may be split into multiple stories or one of many other things.

Refinement may occur in an ad hoc fashion or it may be a regular planned event. Indeed, the variations are endless.

Product Owners may undertake refinement by themselves or with the team. It may be a regular activity, say, once a week; or an ad hoc activity as they comb through the backlog.

Some teams schedule regular refinement sessions, say one each sprint. At these sessions the whole team, or just a few team members, will review and refine backlog items with the Product Owner. Refinement sessions might be meetings in their own right, or they may be part of a pre-planning meeting.

Some teams go even further than this. These teams practice mob-programming.

In mob-programming the whole team—developers, Testers, and Product Owner—sit together and write the product together. The conversation continues until the work is copleted, that is, the story/feature/fix is ready for delivery. This is perhaps the ultimate in story refinement because the final refinement is code and working software.

3 Amigos

Ideally one would hope that every story that is scheduled is clear, concise, has plenty of acceptance criteria, and requires little elaboration. However, there are few perfect stories, and arguably crafting the perfect story is a waste of time—if only because not all stories will be scheduled for development.

As I never tire of repeating: *a story is a placeholder for a conversation.* No matter how imperfect a story is, when it comes to be developed, a conversation needs to be had. Some teams formalize this as a "3-Amigos" meeting—alternatively this is sometimes called a "Power of Three."

3-Amigos occurs immediately before a story is to be developed. The Product Owner, Programmer(s) who will be developing the story, and the Tester meet together to discuss the story, agree acceptance criteria, and generally refine it there and then.

Testing

On teams without a professional Software Tester, the Product Owner will inevitably be called on to perform some testing. But even on teams with a professional Tester, Product Owners should expect to get involved with testing. Ultimately the Tester is a proxy for the Product Owner: Does this story reach the standard required? Does it do the job it set out to do?

There are limits how much the Product Owner can delegate and how much a Tester can know. A quick visual check at a developer's desk can be a very cheap way to get rapid feedback.

As the person responsible for meeting customer needs, the Product Owner sometimes needs to make the call on whether a story, and a product, is ready or not. (And since the Product Owner is often the originator of the story, they are the person who really knows what they were looking for.)

Estimating work items

In general Product Owners should not attach effort estimates to work items. Such estimates are the job of those who will do the estimates in future.

However, Product Owners may request others to provide estimates and they may assign statistical estimates to work items. For example, they may ask the team "How long do you think X will take?", or they may calculate that the average duration of a work item is 6 working days and assign that "estimate."

Of course, there are exceptions. One such exception arises when Product Owners assign all estimates and delivery teams are not expected to honor such estimates. For example, one version of capacity planning asks Product Owners to apportion seriously wild-arsed guesses (SWAG) numbers to work items. The "estimates" are not so much time estimates as capacity bids.

And more to do

The list above is by no means exhaustive; there are more things a Product Owner might need to do. Nor is the list above compulsory; few Product Owners will do all the tasks above. However, for each item above, the Product Owner should know either who is doing the task or why the task does not apply in their setting.

Offstage Product Owner

The power to question is the basis of all human progress.

—Indira Gandhi, Prime Minister of India, 1966–1977, 1980–1984[1]

Hopefully as you were reading that last chapter, you were asking yourself: How does the Product Owner know what to write on a user story? How does the Product Owner know the right acceptance criteria to specify? And how do they know that story X is more valuable than story Z and should therefore be done first?

Knowing the answers to these questions is the reason Product Owners exist. Product Owners are specialists in knowing what should be built, or rather, what customers value.

Descriptions of Scrum and agile focus on what the Product Owner does in the Scrum/agile process with the team. These sources say little about how the Product Owners find out what they need to know. I think of the work Scrum sets out for the Product Owner to do with the team the *onstage work*. This is work that the PO does when they are acting out Scrum but there is much more to the role.

---

[1] Quoted in Dawn Nicole Martin, *In Misbehave: Speak Truth to Power* (Inkwater Press, 2011).

© Allan Kelly 2019
A. Kelly, *The Art of Agile Product Ownership*,
https://doi.org/10.1007/978-1-4842-5168-3_9

When not working directly with the team, much of the Product Owner's time—time the team cannot see—is spent in research (finding things out) and analysis (making sense of what they find). During this time the Product Owner is getting ready to work with the team and ensuring that the work the team will do adds as much value as possible.

Researching and analysis go hand in hand. I'm calling them out as separate activities to make things clearer. Research is finding things out, while analysis is making sense of what you learn. Thinking it through. Turning it over in one's mind. Arguing with oneself. Comparing notes and thinking with peers, triangulating one's own thoughts with those of others. Perhaps using financial models or specific "analysis tools" such as PEST or SWOT. And even, just sleeping on it and seeing if it looks different the next morning.

Some research and analysis will be conducted with the team or team members—and so will be visible. Team members will benefit from visiting and talking with customers, but only the Product Owner can justify doing this routinely. Programmers need to spend most of their time creating programs; observing customers helps inform this process, but their focus is on creation. Similarly, Testers will find meeting customers adds value to their testing work, but to spend more time with customers than tests is hard to justify.

Product Owners will undertake some analysis by themselves, hunched over a spreadsheet or sketching ideas on paper in pen. But some analysis is best shared with other team members, perhaps replacing the pencil and paper with a whiteboard and dry-wipe pen. Figure 9-1 illustrates how some of this work fits together.

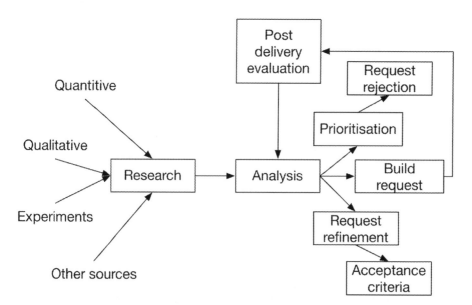

Figure 9-1. Offstage research and analysis allow the Product Owner to do their onstage job

Types of research

Broadly speaking, there are three types of research a PO may undertake: quantitative, qualitative, and experimental.

Quantitative

Quantitative research uses, well, quantities, numbers, statistics, things that might be counted. How many customers does the company have? How many of those customers are under 25? How many have bought in the last 12 months?

Quantitative research may involve analyzing existing data sets, for example, sales transactions, or creating a new data set, for example, running a survey. While numbers have their own authority—"70% of customers over 65 made a repeat purchase in the last 12 months"—they do not tell the full story and can mislead.

Qualitative

Qualitative research describes the quality rather than the quantity. Qualitative tells a story: "our product sells to older customers, every year some die, and some enter institutions where they are unlikely to need our product."

Quantitative data needs qualitative research to both understand the numbers and to know what questions to ask in the first place. Without a qualitative understanding, quantitative measurements are meaningless. Numbers without meaning is like flying over mountains in an airplane and observing the peaks through cloud. Are they mountains 1000 meters tall? Or 2,000? 5000?

Until recently most Business Analyst and Product Management research was qualitative.[2] There was little data available and it was expensive to conduct experiments. Modern technology has changed this.

Online commerce leaves a data trail the way dogs leave footprints in sand. Quantitative data are the exhaust fumes of modern business. While much of this data is useful and holds insights without a qualitative understanding, such data can be highly misleading.

---

[2] I'll give them the benefit of the doubt and assume that none of them ever devised business cases based on technology solutions or pure desk-based dreaming.

Experimental

Hopefully I need not explain experimental research. I hope readers remember back to their school science lessons. I certainly learned to write hypothesis "Sodium dropped into water will burn" and then test the hypothesis myself— or at least watch a teacher conduct the experiment.

Until recently it was simply too expensive for most Product Owners to conduct experiments. Suppose you wanted to find out which shade of blue customers preferred for your product. On a traditional mainframe system, you would be lucky to get to try two shades of blue a year.

On a desktop system, you might be able to change the shade of blue more often, but you still needed to change the shade, recompile the program, perhaps run it through QA, cut it to CD, and ship it. And once you have exposed your customers to the different shades, you need to (quantitatively) find out which they preferred. Then you need a mechanism to get the data back, hopefully one that doesn't take too long.

As a Google Product Manager Marissa Meyer (later Yahoo CEO) famously tested 50 shades of blue for Google to see which customers preferred. Or perhaps more accurately, which shade lead to the most customer interactions.

Modern technology has made it cheap to conduct experiments. Consequently, experimentation has been added to the Product Owners toolkit.

Quantitative, qualitative, or experimental?

Quantitative, qualitative, and experimental approaches to research and analysis are not exclusive. They complement one another rather than compete. Different environments call for different approaches. An online retail may find experimental approaches work well, while a regulated financial service needs to make more use of qualitative techniques.

The promise of experimentation is that it tells you want people actually do, not what they say they will do (as with qualitative). However, experiments need to be conducted carefully and often at a large scale to be valid. Hence, quantitative techniques need to be used to examine the result. A true understanding of the data may only emerge with the additional of qualitative findings.

Meet with customers

There is one form of qualitative research that deserves particular attention: meeting customers.

Or users. Or any other stakeholder.

Every Product Owner should be meeting with customers and understanding what they use the product for. There are few, if any, things more important than meeting customers.

It is also one of the simplest and cheapest techniques to implement. What's not to like?

Because a qualitative understanding of customers and users underpins almost all other forms of research, it is worth looking at some qualitative practices in more detail.[3]

In theory, qualitative research is the easiest and cheapest form of research to conduct: a PO only need walk to a place where there are many potential customers or users and start asking questions.

Walk into the staff canteen, walk up to a random person, and ask, "Excuse me, do you use the XYZ system?"

Walk into the high street and stop a random stranger, then ask, "Excuse me, have you ever used the ABC web site?", or "Do you have the DEF app on your phone?"

So much for theory. Many Product Owners don't want to talk to strangers. Organizations, particularly the sales department, don't want POs talking to customers. Senior Executives fear that POs will divulge a state-secret or promise action the company has not agreed.

And talking to customers can be expensive. Some years ago, I was a Product Manager in London. I wanted to speak to a customer in Finland. Getting to Helsinki took half a day, and another day to get back, actually meeting the customer took up another half day and so an overnight stay was unavoidable.

Almost two days of my time for a two-hour meeting. But what I learned was gold-dust. It led me to understand that the original vision for my product was not one customers shared.

Meeting

When I say meet, I don't just mean meet, introduce yourself, and share a coffee. Product Owners should be seeking to understand

- Who are the customers? What are the different types of customer? What market segment do customers represent?

- What do the customers use the product for?

---

[3] I also fear that with the current popularity of experimental research techniques, some Product Owners are negating first-hand customer contact.

- What would customers do if the product did not exist?

- How does the product improve the customers' life or work?

- How could the product be better?

And probably, right at the bottom of the list:

- What would the customers like the product to do that it does not?

For a planned, formal, customer meeting, the Product Owner may well want to create structured interview to ensure they ask the important questions. Such a questionnaire can be used again and again. Although it is likely that at each asking new insights will reveal new avenues to explore and others to discard.

If a meeting cannot be actually arranged, then a telephone conversation may suffice. Although such calls lose some contextual information, they can still yield valuable insights. Other communication forms—such as e-mail and instant messenger—lack even more context and are not as free flowing as conversation.

While I would accept a telephone call when a physical meeting is not possible, I hesitate to suggest written messages. Such messages can have their place but usually only as short, specific, follow-up questions or for clarification.

Visiting ten customers in a week might not be possible but phone calls—or other remote working tools—may well make it possible to gain a broader understanding. However, some contact should still be physical. Quantity is not always a perfect substitute for quality.

At a very minimum, Product Owners should be meeting customers from time to time to validate that experiments, quantitative studies, and telephone conversations are not missing important details.

Informal meetings

POs should also be on the lookout for informal meetings. User groups and conferences can provide lots of opportunities to meet with actual customers and ask questions. However, such opportunities also present challenges.

You don't want a customer to feel ambushed and you shouldn't bank on having a long conversation. Note taking or recording will probably be difficult, although you may make some notes immediately after the meeting.

Informal meetings may be lubricated with alcohol. While this can make such meetings more enjoyable, it also presents challenges, especially when trying to ask specific questions or recall what was said.

In general POs should be open to the idea of informal customer meetings at any time, you never know when you will fortuitously bump into a customer but that also means one has to know the right questions to ask and when to respect social boundaries.

Observe customers

Observing customers/users in their own environment is another powerful technique. Customers need not be using your product; indeed if your product is completely new, this may not be possible. Your interest may well be "how are things done without the product."

Observing a customer presents more challenges than merely asking them a few questions. For starters it probably takes more time. It is also a more intrusive technique; you will at the very least be sitting in their workspace watching them. In some cases, you may be sitting in their home overseeing them.

Installing cameras to record customer actions would remove the physical intrusion but may be more suspicious because of the events being recorded. Tools are available that use the customer's machine to record the user in action. Such tools can record action, speech, and even video. But, by their nature, they are limited to what happens on the machine and in the immediate vicinity.

Understand the prospective customers

Whether meeting, interviewing, watching, or recording customers, one needs to be constantly trying to see the world as the customer does.

What is it they want to do?

Why do they want to do it?

What problem(s) do they encounter—in general, with your product, with other products they must use?

What opportunities exist to help the customer undertake their task in some better way, whether that be faster, cheaper, easier, or something else?

A Product Owner needs to build empathy with customers and users.

Evaluation

All too frequently Product Owners are so busy adding more stories to the backlog and getting the team to build new stories that they forget to look at what has been delivered and ask: Did it meet our expectations? Did it please users?

Those undertaking experimentation know that an inherent part of the experimentation is to look at what happens and decide what to do next. But actually, the same is true of all work whether it is called an experiment or not.

If a new feature gets built for a specific customer request, shouldn't one ask the customer "did the feature do what you needed?"

If advertising is increased to bring in new customers, surely one should look at customer numbers and ask, "did the adverts work?"

If a set of changes don't deliver the expected results, is it worth doing further planned changes? Or is it with revisiting the changes?

It is vital that new work is evaluated to complete the analysis. Unfortunately, this step is too often overlooked.

Other sources

The above sources are by no means an exhaustive list. There are many more techniques available, and each of those mentioned is worth of an entire book by itself. (I am sure entire books have been written about all of the techniques mentioned so far.) Still, it is worth mentioning a few more techniques.

Support desk

One favorite source of ideas is calls to the support desk. After all, customers who are struggling deserve help and they call or e-mail the support desk everyday with problems which could be solved. However, the support desk can be a very misleading place to look for product ideas.

In general requests which come through the support desk tend to be small incremental changes rather than grand leaps. For some products that is fine but for others it is a blind alley.

More problematic is the type of people who contact the support desk. In general callers fail into one of two groups.

The first group are those new to the product, those who lack experience and who may have been "thrown in the deep end" by an employer. Sometimes you may absolutely want to help people overcome their initial problems with the product, and the right thing to do is to remove each and every obstacle to early use. But many times, that is exactly what you do not want.

The second group who are most likely to contact the support desk are the exact opposite of the first group: the most experienced users. Those who have been using our product for some time and are pushing the boundaries. Consider them the most advanced users.

Again, you might actively want to help this group, you might be trying to make your product the most advanced widget-maker on the market, and those people will help you advance the state of the art. But more often than not, these people will lead you astray. By definition such advanced users constitute a small part of your user base, and satisfying their every need means you will neglect the mass of your users.

For that is the main problem with relying on support desk calls to drive your product: you ignore the mass of customers who do not call the support desk. While you are busy adding features to support new or advanced customers, you are detracting from the time and energy used to support far more customers.

Sales people

If you are developing any kind of product for sale, it is most likely your company employs dedicated sales people.

One of the great things about sales people is that they are very focused on the next customer—for some this can be an obsession. Consequently, when a sales person walks in and says:

> You know, customers want it orange. Orange is the color of today. Everyone wants it orange. Making it orange is the most important thing we can do today.

What they are actually saying is something like:

> The customer who I have just spoken to wants it orange. They really want it orange. I can sell it if it is orange. If you make it orange, I have a sale. (And hence I have my commission.)

Sales people are great because they are customer champions. But that also means they are blind to almost everything else. The next sale is their top priority. After all, that is why your company loves them and why they get sale commission.

The problem is, as a PO—and in particular if you are a Product Manager— your job is to look the market. Your job is not to consider what one customer wants but to consider what customers in aggregate want. And since resources are limited—and you cannot please all the people all the time—your job is to actively decide what is not being done (so that something else can be done).

Saying yes is easy. If the company wants you to say yes to every request, then you might as well resign today because you lack real authority.

Of course, you need to listen to sales people. Of course, you need to consider sales. But your job is more than that.

Competitors

Another common way of coming up with feature ideas is to look at competitor products and copy. Even if you don't start out with this strategy, it is easy to fall into when customers start "feature-shoot-outs" and compare product feature by feature.

As a general rule, you want to avoid feature-shoot-outs. If you are constantly trying to keep feature parity with competitors, then you are constantly playing catch-up. Worse still, your product will become full of features that are seldom used but complicate the user interface and the code base and confuse users.

By all means look at competitors but look at them so you can differentiate your product from theirs. If your competitor genuinely has a similar product which is better—more features, easier to use, faster, etc.—then find a way to make yours different. Perhaps not through technology but perhaps through target market or price point.

In *Crossing the Chasm*, Geoffrey Moore[4] suggests you choose your own competitors. Be ready to say to a customer:

> Yes, I know product Q is often seen as a competitor
> to ours, but we have never considered it a competitor.
> They cater for a different type of customer....

Then be ready with your reason: "they cater to advanced super user," "theirs is an entry level product for small scale operations," "they are a global player with global prices to match," or some other reason.

Reading and scanning

In academic circles there is a step before any experiment, before any case study interviews or survey: the literature review.

---

[4] G. A. Moore, *Crossing the Chasm* (Capstone publishing, 1999).

While customer interviews, data analysis, and experiments in the market can all yield useful information, one should always start from what is already known. There is no point running an experiment to prove that Liverpool FC fans buy more red shirts when it is a well-known fact already.

When researching a market and a product, there may well be specific market reports available which analyze the market. When launching a customer product, there are many review sites which recommend—and forewarn—about existing products.

It can be worth reading the existing literature in a domain. Even if it doesn't directly feed into your product, you will have a better understanding of your customers.

Likewise keeping up with intelligent news and analysis sources can help too. I have lost count of the time I have read something in *The Economist* which has later come in useful with a client.

Every Product Owner is different

While all Product Owners play a key role in deciding what should get built—and communicating that to the delivery team—how they decide and communicate differs massively.

No two Product Owners will work in the same way. The Product Owner role inevitably differs from person to person and place to place. Why would two Product Owners, in different settings, with different teams, different users and customers, work in the same ways?

When not with the team, the Product Owner is getting ready to be with the team. That means meeting customers—or users, or stakeholders—and finding out what they need. That information needs to be combined with other information—perhaps market growth reports, or sales figures, or company targets. Some of this will happen on paper, some on whiteboards or with other tools. But it will all happen inside the Product Owners mind.

The first thing every newly appointed Product Owner needs to do is to decide: how they will play the role and, most importantly, how they will find out the things they need to know to write stories, prioritize the backlog, work with the team, etc.

Many of the research and analysis tools deployed by Product Owners come straight from existing Business Analysis and Product Management playbooks. Later chapters look more at the Product Owner role itself and what Product Owners can learn from Business Analysts and Product Managers.

The Busy Product Owner

Life is what happens to you while you're busy making other plans.

—John Lennon, "Beautiful Boy (Darling Boy)," Geffen Records, 1980

One aspect in particular of the Product Owner role really annoys me: they have so much work to do.

Or rather, a Product Owners who is doing their job properly—as opposed to simply administering the backlog—has so many things they should potentially be doing.

Consider the following responsibilities.

- Backlog administration: Writing stories, reviewing and discussing suggested stories, splitting stories, weeding the backlog (throwing stories away), improving stories, putting value on stories, writing acceptance criteria

- Working with the team: Talking to the stories, reviewing work in progress, reviewing "completed" work, potentially signing-off or formally accepting stories, participating in 3-Amigos meetings with Testers and developers, helping to improve the development processes

© Allan Kelly 2019
A. Kelly, *The Art of Agile Product Ownership*,
https://doi.org/10.1007/978-1-4842-5168-3_10

- User Experience Design/Interface Design: Working even more closely with UXD specialists because the two roles overlap, and possibly substituting for UXD specialists where they are absent

- Meetings: Prioritization pre-planning meeting, planning meeting themselves, stand-up meetings, retrospectives, show and tell demonstrations (potentially delivering them the show and tell themselves)

- Interfacing to the wider organization: Reporting and listening to internal stakeholders in authority, attending governance and/or portfolio review meetings, aligning product strategy and plans with company strategy and plans, plus feeding back to company strategy about their own product strategy and plans

- Planning: Participating in sprint planning with the team, planning for upcoming iterations (the rolling quarter plan as I like to call it), longer-term planning which might take the form of a roadmap, a capacity plan, a scenario plan, or all three.

  - Customers 1: Identifying customers and potential customer, segmenting the customer base, creating customer profiles and personas

  - Customers 2: Visiting customers, observing customers, talking to customers about stories and potential future work, reflecting on customer comments, and feeding back to the team and other stakeholders

  - Customers 3: Similar activities to number two with people and organizations who are not currently customers but who are potential customers (because potential customers who have unmet needs represent growth)

I'm sure some of you are saying: "But we don't have external customers, we have internal (captive) users." And you're right, if you have such "customers," then you have a subset of these activities. But then again, shouldn't you be thinking about how our product is used by internal users to service the needs of external customers? And how you could improve that experience (for the customers) and improve the process (for the users)?

- Marketing: Inbound marketing the items just mentioned under customers plus market scanning (checking out the competitors) and potentially outbound marketing (advertising, PR, trade shows, etc.)

- Sharing expert knowledge: Providing knowledge about the domain and subject of development to the development team, supporting sales calls, demonstrating the product at shows (and when the company is small, helping the training and support teams)

- The offering: Using the information gained in all these activities to refine the product/service offering to satisfy customers or improve business processes: Is it the right offering? Are you targeting the right customer segment? Should you be offering something else?

- Close the loop: Evaluating the effect on customers and/or process: Are the features being used? Are non-feature improvements making a difference? What shouldn't have been done? What arises from the changes that have been made? More software changes? Process changes?

- Money: Is all this making money? Is the continued existence of the team positive to ROI?

This is not to say that all Product Owners should be doing all of these things. Asking one person to take all this on is probably setting them up to fail. Every Product Owner should recognize every item on this list. If they aren't doing any of these items themselves, then I expect they can either cross it off (doesn't need doing where they work) or name the person who is doing it.

And I also expect every Product Owner can add some things to this list which I have overlooked.

Stop Doing

One's philosophy is not best expressed in words; it is expressed in the choices one makes.

—Eleanor Roosevelt (1884–1962)

Even a quick look at the list of potential actives in the last chapter will tell you the Product Owner is going to be a busy person. Fortunately, there are some things that Product Owners can stop doing—something they might be able to stop immediately and some others they should work toward dropping.

It is worth repeating what I said earlier about time: If Product Owners do not have time to do their jobs properly, specifically if they do not have enough time to visit customers, question and listen to customers, and do not have time to analyze the results of those meetings and reflect those learning in their backlogs and prioritization, then, in time, the work they prioritize will reduce in value. Opinion will substitute for well-researched facts; quick knee-jerk prioritization decisions will be made over well-considered choices, and over time the work being done will decline in value.

No coding

Product Owners' cutting code should NOT be cutting code.

Having a former coder in the Product Owner role can be a great boom. Not only do they know how to talk with the technical team and (hopefully) can command their respect, but they can also see how technology can apply.

© Allan Kelly 2019
A. Kelly, *The Art of Agile Product Ownership*,
https://doi.org/10.1007/978-1-4842-5168-3_11

But to be an effective Product Owner, they need to step away from the keyboard and stop writing code.

Two reasons: first, time. Product Owners add value by ensuring that the code which is written addresses the most valuable opportunities in the smallest, most elegant, delightful way possible. Every minute spent coding is a minute not doing that.

Second: Product Owners need to empathize with the customer, with the business users, they need to eat-sleep-and-breath customers.

Being a good coder—let alone someone called an architect—is to empathize with code, the system, the mechanics of how a system works.

Importantly both requirements and code need to be able to come together and discuss what they see and find a way to bring the two—sometimes opposing—views together. It is a lot easier to have that discussion if the two sides are represented by different people.

Asking one person to divide their brain in two and discuss opposing views with themselves is unlikely to bring about the best result and is probably a recipe for confusion and stress.

That's not to say both sides shouldn't appreciate the other. As I said before, former coders have a great advantage in being a Product Owner. And I want the technical team to meet customers. But I want discussions to be between two (or more) people. I might allow an exception here for Minimally Viable Teams, but once the team moves beyond the MVT stage, the PO should stop coding.

No line management

Product Owners should NOT be line managers.

OK, senior Product Owners should might line manage junior Product Owners, but they certainly should not be line managing anyone else. Most certainly they should not be line managing the technical team.

Product Owner authority comes not from a line on an organization chart, or the ability to award (or deny) a pay rise or bonus. Product Owner authority stems from their specialist knowledge of what customers want from a product and what the organization considers valuable.

If the Product Owner cannot demonstrate their specialist knowledge in this way, then either they should learn fast or they should consider if they are in the right role.

Product Owners need to trust the technical team and the technical team need to trust the Product Owner. Authority complicates this relationship because one side is allowed to issue orders when trust is absent, and the other side has to obey.

And again, Product Owners simply don't have the time to line manage anyone.

Being a good line manager requires empathy with employees and time to spend observing and talking to employees, helping them develop themselves, helping them with problems, and so on.

Product Owners should not make promises for other people to keep.

Specifically, that means they should not issue "roadmaps" which list features with delivery dates based on effort estimates. The whole issue of estimation is a minefield, very few teams are in a position to estimate accurately, and most humans are atrocious at time estimation anyway. So, any plans based on effort estimation are a fantasy anyway. But even putting that to one side…

Issuing such plans commits other people to keep promises. That is just unfair.

Product Owners can create and share scenario plans about how the product—and world—might unfold in the future.

Product Owners can co-create and share capacity plans which should how an organization intends (strategically) to allocate resources. And Product Owners can work with teams in executing against those capacity plans in order to deliver functionality the Product Owner thinks should be delivered by a date the Product Owner thinks is necessary.

In other words, provided a Product Owner is making the promise that they intend to keep themselves (i.e., they have skin in the game), then they might issue some kind of forward plan.

Dump outbound marketing

Product Owners should dump outbound marketing at the first opportunity.

Outbound marketing, for example, advertising, press releases, public relations, and product evangelism, often ends up on the Product Owner plate—particularly when the Product Owner is a Product Manager. And in a small company (think early stage start-up), this just needs to be accepted.

However, in a larger organization, or a growing start-up, Product Owners should seek to pass this work to a dedicated Product Marketing specialist as soon as possible. Both roles deserve enough time to do the job properly.

The Marketing Specialist and Product Owner will work closely together—they are after all two sides of the same coin, the Marketing coin. The Marketing Specialist handles outbound marketing (telling people about the product), and the Product Owner handles inbound marketing (what do people want from the product?). (Again, in organizations with established Product Management, this is usually easier to see. See later chapters for more discussion of Product Management and marketing.)

Dump pre-sales

Product Owners should dump pre-sales at the first opportunity.

As with outbound marketing, Product Owners often get dragged in as pre-sales support to account managers. And again, this is more common in small companies and early stage start-ups.

There are some advantages to playing second fiddle to a sales person. The Product Owner will get actual customer contact (sales people too often block product people from meeting customers.) And Product Owners should be exposed to some of the commercial pressures that sales people—and customers—encounter.

But doing pre-sales is very time consuming. And being wheeled in to help deliver a sale will distort the Product Owner's view of the market—just because this customer wants the product in orange doesn't mean other customers want orange.

Once infront of a customer the Product Owner will come under pressure to commit to particular requests and make promises against dates. These pressures arise both from the customer and sales person but also from them-selves because they want to please people. Unfortunately, once a customer's (or sales person's) expectations have been set, it is hard to backtrack even if other work is more valuable.

And again, pre-sales are more effectively done by specialist staff as soon as the company can afford them.

Avoid the writing trap

Product Owners are often tempted to add more detail to their stories. In fact, they are often asked by Programmers and Testers to provide more detail. However, this is a trap best avoided. Rather than more writing, Product Owners should provide more conversation.

An old agile maxim says:

> Write slightly less than you think is needed.

If a PO writes less than is needed, then someone can ask a question and a conversation can follow. The written word seldom adds as much as a conversation because writing is one way, from the writer to the reader. And the message is decided not by the writer but by the reader.

In contrast, a conversation allows both parties to ask questions and iterate until a shared understanding is reached.

The pressures to write more can be intense: outsourced delivery teams, remote teams, regulators, audit trails, and governance all add to the pressure. But remember writing is very expensive for both the writer and the reader. Well actually, it is only expensive for the reader if there is a reader; if nobody ever reads the written words, then it is complete waste.

Specialist Help

Alone we can do so little; together we can do so much.

—Helen Keller[1]

I explained that there was an awful lot of work for a Product Owner to do, then I suggested some things a Product Owner should NOT be doing, next I suggested how the role can be refactored to reduce the workload. Now I'd like to suggest some more ways a Product Owner can reduce their workload.

More importantly, what follows is not just advice for reducing the workload; this advice can help Product Owners do a better job by involving more people, getting more views and more expertise involved.

Use the team

In the old days, it was not uncommon to see an "Us and Them" relationship between those charged with understanding business and customer ("us") and those tasked with building the product ("them").

This was made worse when there were multiple people in each role, for example, a team of Business Analysts working together to product requirements for a team of developers. It is also made worse when these teams—or just individuals in roles—work in physically different places (and maybe never meet) or work for different organizations, say the Client and the Supplier.

---

[1] Quoted in Lash Joseph P., *Helen and Teacher: The Story of Helen Keller and Anne Sullivan Macy* (Delacorte Press/Seymour Lawrence, 1980).

© Allan Kelly 2019
A. Kelly, *The Art of Agile Product Ownership*,
https://doi.org/10.1007/978-1-4842-5168-3_12

One way "Us and Them" manifested itself was a battle of the documentation.

Needless to say, in the perfect world of agile, this never happens: teams are co-located, friendly, work to the same goal, and don't write anything down.

Well, yes, it does happen in some places.

But simply waving the agile-wand doesn't make it so. There are plenty of teams out there who are nominally agile but where the "Us and Them" business vs. technical divide still exists.

Unfortunately, this makes more work or the business/requirements people—energy to maintain the divide, the extra formality, documentation, and arguments required.

Product Owners should see the technical delivery team not as their enemy but as their partner—there should after all be one team. The delivery team are clever people who know technology, may well have built similar things before, and may have some understanding of the business domain.

Even if they don't, they are another pair of eyes (usually many pairs of eyes).

When the Product Owner trusts the members of the delivery team, they reduce their own workload and that of the team. They need to give them less detail in their requests (they trust the team to ask questions), they practice less management (they ask for less reports and listen to fewer), they agonize, question, and gossip about the team less.

Product Owners need to enroll the team, take them to meet customers, have them talk to stakeholders, hold joint backlog weeding sessions, have them review stories and comment on them, and delegate work to team members.

Unless delivery members are involved in discussions and conversations with customers, they are unlikely to ever properly understand "the business."

Testing specialist

Following directly from that last point, as Product Owners find more and more of their time devoted reviewing work and testing, the greater the value in adding a specialist Tester to help. Of course, the Product Owner must be prepared to delegate authority to the specialist Tester to accept work. If they are not prepared to delegate that authority, then they need to keep testing themselves.

This also elevates the professional Testers role: they are less concerned with "pressing return 50 times to see if it crashes" and more concerned with "ensuring it delivers benefit to the users/customers."

In many ways Professional Testers start to look more like Product Owners: they too try to understand what the customer is trying to achieve and are tasked with ensuring the customer's world really is a better place with the new tools and whether product enhancements deliver the expected benefits. When enhancements don't deliver the expected benefits, it is time to ask: What else can be done? How can that value be unlocked? Or perhaps, was the expectation misplaced? There is no point in doing more work to unlock an expected benefit when the benefit doesn't exist or is far smaller than anticipated.

In some cases, a professional Tester may well be the first to see new opportunities which arise. Naturally they should feedback such insights to the Product Owner. One can expect the roles of Product Owner and professional Tester to increasingly overlap.

User experience/interface specialists

In many, probably most, teams, little or no attention is paid to the user interface design. The Programmers "throw" together something. Some Programmers are good at this, and sometimes—frankly—a crude programmer-designed interface is good enough.

In many environments the interface design skills of Programmers will be quite adequate. That is not to say the result will be impressive let alone intuitive, rather it is to recognize that in many places, impressive and intuitive interfaces are simply not required or justified.

Consider an internal application for managing supplier invoices. Such system may only be used by a handful of people for a dozen invoices a week. It might be painful for an accountant to use, and there might be benefits to creating an Apple-quality interface, but would a system enhancement add value? Would it add enough value to justify the cost of the work? Or would the same effort be better directed to work with greater benefit?

But sometimes quality user interfaces are entirely justified. Indeed, too many companies settle for a "good enough" Programmer-designed interface when well-considered professionally designed experience would unlock significant value. This is particularly true of products which will be marketed and sold to external customers.

When the needs for user interface and interaction move beyond the skills of the programming team, it usually lands on the Product Owner's desk. (And this happens a lot sooner when the Product Owner doesn't trust the delivery team.)

So many Product Owners end up, for better or worse, "designing" (or simply mandating) the look and feel of the Product. While some are good at this—they have an eye for design and might have done this before—most of them are little better than the Programmers who throw things together.

Unfortunately, when Product Owners are also interface designers, discussions about user interface can obscure the problem or opportunity the Product Owner is trying to address. Rather than talking about what the user is trying to achieve, discussion centers on how the user will accomplish the task. Such debates—particularly when conducted in writing—can get acrimonious and time consuming.

Sometimes the User Interface, the Interaction Experience, the Design, the Look and Feel, the…whatever you call it…make A VERY BIG DIFFERENCE. On these occasions it is worth having specialists in interface design on the team. Such specialists might be called interface designers, user experience designers (UXD), or just designers.

Sometimes it is the way a product works which is the thing that differentiates the product and makes it a winner. Consider Apple.

At the time of writing (mid-2019), Apple is one of the world's most valuable companies. One of the major reasons for Apple success is their respect for the user and their efforts to product systems and interfaces which not only look good but are (relatively) easier to use than their competitors.

Apple does not get it right every time—this writer constantly finds iTunes frustrating to use. And Apple does not always get it right first time or produce killer products every time (consider Apple TV). But Apple does engage in significant customer research and user observation—frequently hidden from view.[2]

While few companies have the financial resources to devote to design what Apple does, in my experience, almost every company would benefit in spending more money on user experience design even if it means reducing expenditure on programming.

Obviously, when the interface makes a big difference, or when the Product Owner is spending a lot of time on interface design—or when the Product Owner lacks the skills to take on the work—then it is time to add an UXD specialist.

And there is another lesson from UXD…

In many ways a UXD specialist is one of "Us"—they will have insights into customers' needs, they will work closely with the Product Owner in deciding what needs to be done and how to satisfy the need. But a UXD specialist is also one of "Them"—they are part of the delivery process, they are a technical specialist, they are there to be instructed in what to do next.

---

[2] In June 2019—while this book was being finalized—Apple announced that iTunes was to split into three different apps.

Even more than the professional Tester, the UXD role highlights the absurdity of Product Owners seeing an "Us and Them" relationship with those creating the product. The very difficulty in pigeon-holing UXD demonstrates why pigeon-holing is a stupid idea.

When I say UXD, I mean User Experience Design, but these comments apply equally if you prefer the term UX, Interface Design, and other variations of this term. What I mean is the activity of, and professionals who consider, how a user works with the system. Both analysis of the way people work with the machine/system and the synthesis of products to improve interaction. I am taking a liberty by using these terms almost interchangeably here.

Finally, UXD specialists do not only help Product Owners by removing some of the work POs have to do. Most UXD experts are themselves trained and experienced in observing customers and understanding their problems and needs. As such UXD are another pair of eyes and partners in understanding users.

The default dogs' body

As always, there is a lot of work the Product Owner could, even should, be doing. Frequently when there is no specialist available, the Product Owner becomes the default dogs' body to pick up the work nobody else wants to do—or lacks the time to do.

Sometimes this is necessary, in a start-up company or a minimally viable team. But this can also be self-inflicted. Product Owners who don't trust their team members may feel they need to take on responsibilities—like UXD—themselves.

With success and additional resources, Product Owners should seek to offload some of their work to specialists. Not only will these specialists free up the Product Owner time, but they will do a better job than a time-pressed Product Owner who has never worked as a user-experienced designer or software Tester.

When additional resources are available, the tyranny of the backlog can lead Product Owners—and the organization as a whole—to prioritize more coders rather than specialists. Yet frequently the right specialists can add more value than another Programmer. This is especially true in the case of user experience/interface design. Just ask Apple.

Role Models

Right at the start of this book, I wrote:

> Every Product Owner needs to work out what is right the right way for them to fill the Product Owner role. Every organization is different. Every team is different, and every individual is different.
>
> For a newly appointed Product Owner, the first job is to sit down and decide what type of Product Owner they will be. Both what the organization expects of them and what type of Product Owner they want to be.

One way of considering this question is to look for role models from which a Product Owner can beg, borrow, and steal. In this section I'd like to look at some role models and ask:

- What can a Product Owner learn from these roles?
- Are these roles alternatives to the Product Owner role?

While there are several role models to consider, two deserve more attention than others: Product Manager and Business Analyst. Since these roles are similar, but different, this is an interesting exercise in its own right. But for a Product Owner, and in particular for someone new to the role of Product Owner, it is helpful for two reasons:

- Product Owners may need to work with Business Analysts and/or Product Managers.
- Product Owners who don't have a background in these roles will need to learn some of the skills and thinking of these roles.

Too many Product Owners are little more than backlog administrators. When this happens, the role adds little value. The Product Owner is limited in what they can do and opportunities to add value are missed.

Product Owners need to be more than just backlog administrators. Product Managers and Business Analysts provide useful role models and demonstrate many of the skills and attitudes great Product Owners need to create great products and add value. Indeed, many of the best Product Owners I meet were once Business Analysts or Product Managers. These people bring valuable skills and experience to the Product Owner role.

Product Owner as Entrepreneur

Product Owners at Revolut lead innovation and growth. They are in charge of building the infrastructure and launching new products and features. ... If a person has complete ownership over a product and sees it through from conception to completion, we feel that the term "owner" is a much better fit. ...

Great products are born out of passion and dedication. We believe that the key to success is the perfect combination of freedom and responsibility that makes a Product Owner feel like they're really owning the whole thing.

—Nik Storonsky[1]

One frequently hears Product Owners compared to entrepreneurs. In start-ups and single-product companies, it is common to find the founder, and CEO, is indeed the Product Owner. It is almost axiomatic that in the beginning there is one leader, one visionary, and there is no need to differentiate between these different roles.

---

[1] Nik Storonsky, "Should Product Owners Think Like Entrepreneurs," Revolut Blog, May 2019, https://blog.revolut.com/should-product-owners-think-like-entrepreneurs/.

© Allan Kelly 2019
A. Kelly, *The Art of Agile Product Ownership*,
https://doi.org/10.1007/978-1-4842-5168-3_13

In larger organizations, where the Product Owner is potentially one of many leaders then one needs to ask: Which attributes of an entrepreneur should the Product Owner emulate? And are there some which are better not copied?

Inspiration

When you think "Entrepreneur" who do you think of? Who is your role model? Perhaps Elon Musk or Richard Branson. Maybe you work for a founding entrepreneur. Or maybe you've only seen people who want to be entrepreneurs on TV—*Shark Tank* or *Dragon's Den*.

What attributes do you associate with such people?

Entrepreneurs succeed for different reasons:

- Steve Jobs was demanding, could read a market, and had an eye for style.

- Bill Gates was a talented Programmer with vision and drive, and he was in the right place at the right time and took risks.

- Larry Page and Sergey Brin had a brilliant idea and were immensely talented engineers.

Typically, entrepreneurs are thought to have passion and vision, they understand their market, they are self-motivated and are great motivators of other people. In their work they are determined, optimistic, risk-takers, who work hard—long hours are expected; they are flexible and "do what is needed." Certainly, you don't expect an entrepreneur to say: "Not my job, governor."

These are all attributes that are desirable in a Product Owner too. At a very minimum, Product Owners need to understand where their product is going. Having their own vision and passion for their product is even better.

One characteristic seldom linked to entrepreneur is administration, even planning might be a stretch, but Product Owners frequently need both skills.

The flip side

When a Product Owner is not an entrepreneur, some of these characteristics might become hindrances. A risk happy PO inside a large corporation might find they are out of step with peers and the expectations of superiors.

Within a corporation, patience, planning, and administrative ability might be key to getting resources and winning arguments.

The vision and passion exhibited by entrepreneurs can be at odds with the explorative hypothesis-driven nature of modern product discovery. A PO with passion and vision might be blind to evidence which invalidates the vision.

I once worked with an agile Coach called Benjamin. He was asked to help an entrepreneur with a vision for a new energy product. Benjamin started discussing minimal viable products—everyone loves minimal viable products—and hypothesis testing. The entrepreneur didn't see the need to test his hypothesis; he was sure he knew what the market wanted. Hypothesis testing was unnecessary, even a waste of time and money. By even raising the question Benjamin had proved himself unsuitable. The entrepreneur wanted his vision realized quickly, and cheaply, agile and Benjamin were supposed to deliver that without too many questions.

Entrepreneurs frequently face doubters and nay sayers. Those that preserve and succeed are held up as great successes in the face of adversity. One might argue that if the entrepreneur's vision was obvious, then someone would have done it already and there would be no market. But for every entrepreneur who succeeds against the odds may more fail.

In a market economy, failure is always an option for entrepreneurs. Indeed, the independent limited liability company was a key invention for modern economies. The ability of an entrepreneur to try, to fail, and then walk away to try another day is fundamental to the way entrepreneurs work.

Corporations are often failure averse; any question of failure and the initiative will not be funded. In such organizations prospective Product Owners much radiate success.

Ownership

When you boil all this down, the common theme is, well, ownership.

Think of home ownership: there are joys in ownership—you get to decorate as you like! But responsibilities too, you have to maintain it. Most of all, ownership means there is nobody else to blame; the buck stops here.

Maybe entrepreneurship and full ownership lie at one end of a spectrum (Figure 13-1). At the other end of the spectrum are backlog administrators who have limited authority. Most Product Owners are somewhere in between. Many might be more correctly termed product custodians.

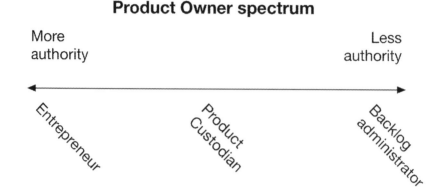

Figure 13-1. The amount of authority determines the type of Product Owner

Product custodians are responsible for a product. But custodianship is limited, most likely by time; sooner or later the custodian will move on and someone else will take their place. If a custodian performs poorly, that time might come to an end sooner than expected.

Like engineers Product Owners work within constraints: resources are restricted, authority only goes so far, and time is limited. Every Product Owner needs to operate within a context; while they can aspire for more authority, more resources, and more freedom, such things often need to be earned.

While one might like to think that entrepreneurs' control everything—and so should a Product Owner!—the truth is entrepreneurs are often constrained. Entrepreneurs are constrained by a lack of resources—think about cash-strapped start-ups. More importantly entrepreneurs are constrained by what customers, the market, will accept and pay for.

Thinking of a Product Owner as an entrepreneur, custodian, or backlog administrator helps understand the mindset required, but it does little to describe the skills required. For that it helps to examine two closely related roles: Product Managers and Business Analysts.

The Product Manager Role

> *People will never love a product that you do not love. If you do not love it yourself, they feel it ... they smell it.*
>
> —Steve Wozniak, Apple Co-founder[1]

The Product Manager role is an inbound marketing role. It is about understanding customers, their needs and their problems. Product Managers seek to understanding what will help customers make progress with their own job and bring joy into their lives. Next, they are communicating this understanding—and the implications—to others, specifically the development team.

The defining feature of the Product Manager role is that their customers are not in the building. Customers are external to the Product Managers organization. Notice I say customers not users, this is deliberate, there is a commercial transaction here. Customers use the product, or service built on the product, and in return money gets paid.

While a Product Manager is primarily concerned with customers outside the building, there are people "in the building" who the Product Manager needs to listen to and work with. Product Managers need to also consider how

---

[1] Quoted in Roberto Verganti, *Overcrowded* (MIT Press, 2016).

© Allan Kelly 2019
A. Kelly, *The Art of Agile Product Ownership*,
https://doi.org/10.1007/978-1-4842-5168-3_14

customers access the product and the end-to-end customer experience. This is especially true when the product is a service.

Although Product Managers have the word "Manager" in their title, they do not manage people, they manage things.[2] Rather they manage the working out of what will get built. Their power rests on their legitimacy and knowledge rather than their direct authority.

Product Managers historically work at companies which produce and sell software products, so-called software vendors, or independent software vendors (ISVs). Companies like Microsoft or Adobe, Oracle, and Intuit. In recent years these companies have moved from selling software—usually on a CD—to selling the software as a service via the Internet.

Software as a service (SaaS) companies such as SalesForce, Google, Facebook, and Twitter use the same model of Product Management.

The dumping ground

In many ways the natural home of Product Management—and the source of many good role models—is Palo Alto, California. While the Product Manager role is long established in the United States—specifically Silicon Valley—it is relatively new in Europe, and I assume elsewhere. As a result, Product Managers, and those who work with Product Managers, are often unsure what the role entails.

One of the problems poor understanding of the Product Manager—and Product Owner—role creates is that the roles become a catchall dumping ground for the things other people don't want to do. That the title includes the word "manager" is part of the problem. The "manager" moniker is never clearly defined. Programmers program, Testers test, Business Analysts, well, analyze, but managers? The title manager always introduces some ambiguity.

If anything, there is even more confusion over the title Product Owner. After all, how does one own a thing? What are owners responsible for? And what do owners do?

Agile has further obscured the true responsibilities of a Product Manager. Some agile advocates go around disparaging managers of any type without. This attitude fails to recognize that some "managers" are actually specialists not administrators or controllers.

These agile advocates have a particular dislike of Project Managers. I have once heard a well-known agile advocate proclaim "There is no place in Scrum for a Project Manager. If you have a Project Manager on a Scrum team you are

---

[2] Of course, it is possible that a Senior Product Manager also line-manages more junior Product Managers.

not doing Scrum." Faced with these attitudes, organizations sometimes remove the Project Manager role naively.

Removing the Project Manager role does not remove all the work the Project Manager was doing. While some work does vanish, other work gets dispersed to the delivery team, and some ends up with the Product Owner/Manager. Elsewhere Project Managers are renamed Product Owner without the actual role changing much. (Other Project Managers get renamed Scrum Masters without a proper understanding of that role either.)

There is a fundamental difference between Project Managers and Product Managers/Owners:

Project Managers are primarily concerned with the when: their role focuses on delivering a pre-defined thing.

Product Managers (and Product Owners) are primarily concerned with the what: their role focuses on deciding what the right thing to build is, both in the short term and the long term.

Consider again the traditional iron triangle introduced earlier—Figure 1-1 in Chapter 1.

Most Project Manager training addresses the schedule and cost dimensions. The assumption is the scope (i.e., the "what shall we build?" question) is already known and fixed. When software Project Managers try to work in the quality dimension, the results can be negative. "It doesn't need to be perfect" proclamations are likely to both reduce Programmer motivation and create more defects which later delay work.

A second major difference comes from authority. Many Project Managers command authority over team members; they can give direct orders. Product Managers and Owners derive their authority from their specialist expertise. Therefore, Product Managers need the respect of the team. Respect needs to be earned, not imposed.

Inbound and outbound marketing

My guess is that when I say marketing most readers immediately think of publicity, advertising, public relations, mail shots, and so on. Marketing tells people you they have something to sell. This is but one aspect to market: outbound marketing.

Outbound marketing is concerned with telling people—potential customers—that your company exists, that you have a product (or service), that that product would be good for them, that they will benefit from the product, and that they should part with money for your product.

But there is another side to marketing. This side exists in all marketing textbooks but receives less attention: inbound marketing. The two sides are shown graphically in Figure 14-1.

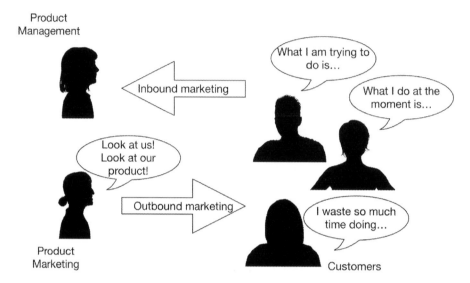

Figure 14-1. Inbound marketing is about understanding customers, their needs, their problems, and what would help them. Outbound marketing is letting them know you can help

Inbound marketing is about discovering what customers need and what they will find valuable. Once inbound marketing has done its job and found the need, then, after the product has been created, outbound marketing comes into play to tell customers that the product exists. Ideally, inbound marketing defines the product so well that customers don't need much persuasion, the product fits their need like a well-made glove, and they are only too pleased to buy.

Product Management is at heart an inbound marketing role: understanding the need. The outbound role is often called Product Marketing.

The Product Marketing function often filled by Product Marketing Managers. They aim to communicate to customers that the product exists and the benefit of the product. They use advertising, public relations, press releases, online web sites, and other media.

The two activities are close—almost opposite sides of a coin—but different. It is hardly surprising that Product Managers are often called on to help with Product Marketing. This is particularly true at small companies who might not be able to afford an additional role. With growth a dedicated Product Marketing Manager can take over outbound responsibilities.

Even when the activities and roles are separate, Product Managers are never very far from Product Marketing and are often the public face of the product. They may be asked to speak at conferences or to the press and they may need to advise on how the product is presented in marketing literature.

To complicate things, the Product Manager role practiced by successful software companies and described here is different to the Product Manager found in many non-technology companies. The role of Product Manager at a company like Proctor & Gamble is an outbound marketing role, one usually involved with brand management. In an effort to differentiate these roles, the title Technical Product Manager has been used in the past. But this change leads some to believe Technical Product Managers are in some way involved with the program code.

Remember the Product Manager

Without a Product Manager directing the direction of development, the success of a commercial product is down to luck and chance. Product Managers are the people who take the luck out of developing software products.

Product Management is not a misunderstood role, it is more an overlooked role. Too many software companies are either ignorant of what good product management can do for them or they believe that developers know best.

If you work at a software company which sells its products—either shrink wrapped or online via a web service—to multiple customers, then you need Product Managers working with the development team.

What Do Product Managers Do?

Over the past several years, I've noticed a change in our industry, … The change is that the vast majority of Product Managers that I meet have had almost no real training at all, and the training they have had is usually a CSPO (Certified Scrum Product Owner) course which doesn't even scratch the surface of what a Product Manager needs to know.

—Marty Cagan[1]

Product Managers work with the development team, with customers, senior managers, and sales and keep watch on technology advances and the wider market, including competitors. They are at the center of many conversations. They attempt to synthesize all they learn into a long-term direction for their product and short-term list of improvements.

---

[1] Marty Cagan, "CEO of the Product Revisited," March 31, 2018, https://svpg.com/ceo-product-revisited/.

© Allan Kelly 2019
A. Kelly, *The Art of Agile Product Ownership*,
https://doi.org/10.1007/978-1-4842-5168-3_15

Product Managers need skills of listening, communicating, sharing, and analysis. Plus, they need commercial skills to understand the financial aspects of their decisions. It is the different requests, demands, constraints, opportunities, and such that form the raw material of their work. As Figure 15-1 shows, a Product Manager is involved in lots of diverse conversations.

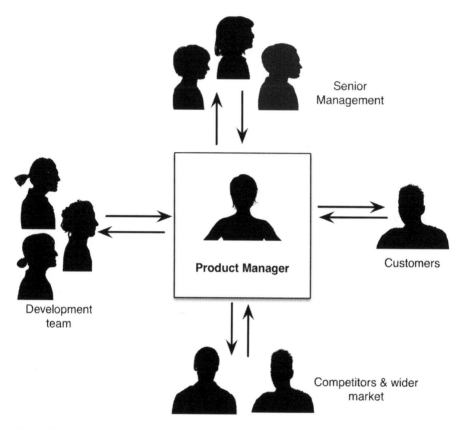

Figure 15-1. Product Manager sits in the center of many conversations

Customers

Product Managers are less concerned with what one individual customer wants and more concerned with what the market wants. Markets are customers in aggregate; in a market there are many customers and potential customers. Customers have many things in common—otherwise they would not form a collective market—but they also have differences. Indeed, defining and shaping a market can be key to winning.

By definition customers are external so Product Managers need to get out into the market to meet customers. They look to find common and reoccurring problems shared by customers and potential customers.

There is something of a chicken-and-egg problem here. Until a Product Manager decides who their customers are, then they don't know who to get out and meet. But until Product Managers meet customers, they can't define who they should meet.

The answer, as with so much else, is iteration. Do a little (meet some customers), think (refine their market view), do a little more... and repeat. Since the market is not static even when the view becomes stable, it needs to be periodically rechecked.

In identifying the customer base, Product Managers will segment customers into groups, for example, home users and business users. Such segments are dynamic and will change over time. It should be possible to identify which segment any given customer belongs in.

Product Managers look for the common problem or *Job to be Done* to use a more recent model.[2] The aim is to create a product which multiple customers will want to buy.

To understand customers Product Managers traditionally meet customers. They may interview them one on one, observe customers using the software, or run focus group discussions. They may undertake surveys, competitor analysis, market scanning and analysis; they may assist sales people and perform win-loss analysis, attend trade shows, and more.

At times—particularly during delivery—a Product Manager may choose to focus on just one customer. Sometimes it is too hard to please all the people and a better approach is to focus on delighting one customer. This can bring great focus. Delighting just one customer may make many other, similar, customers really happy. After the first delighted customer, it is time to focus on customer number two, then number three, and so on.

Product Managers aim to build a product and then have customers buy—or rent—the product. Cashflow will be the ultimate judge of their success.

New technologies are changing the way Product Managers work. The next chapter will discuss some of these changes in more depth.

---

[2] Clayton M. Christensen, *Competing against Luck* (Harper Collins, 2016); C. M. Christensen et al., "Finding the Right Job For Your Product," *Sloan Management Review* 48, no. 3 (Spring 2007): 38–47.

Development team

Product Managers work with technical teams to build the thing they think customers want and will pay for. Consequently, it is common to find the Product Owner role staffed by a Product Manager in a software vendor.

There is no point in Product Managers learning all about customer needs if they don't feed this back to the development team. Some of this is formal feedback—User Stories, for example—and some is informal, conversations over coffee perhaps.

It is in working with the development team that the Scrum Product Owner role is to the fore. These are two-way conversations, during which the Product Manager tells the team what customers need and listens to how the team propose to address the need and what the latest technologies are capable of.

And when I say conversation, I do not mean a single event in time. I mean ongoing dialogue over days, weeks, months, and even years.

Product Managers/Owners specify the goal: they should not propose solutions, and neither should they get involved in technical design. They can be part of the conversation about possible solutions, and they may express a preference for one solution over another. It is a conversation with aspects of negotiation.

This is particularly true when a solution makes a difference to how customers relate to the product. For example, a Product Manager would not review alternative database schema designs, but they would review and comment on different user interface designs. One is visible to the final customer and the other invisible.

Product Managers continue the dialogue about what customer need as the product gets built. Developers come and ask for clarification, "Do you mean this? Or that?" Teams may consult the Product Manager whenever there is a question that will make a difference to how the product functions to the customer.

When products have a non-trivial user interface, development teams should include a user interface designer or user experience designer. In matters of UI design and operation, they will deputize for the Product Manager on UI decisions. In the absence of a UI designer, these kinds of decisions will probably fall to the Product Manager rather than a developer. Unless, of course, a developer also has design skills.

In addition to the specific and immediate goals, Product Managers talk to the development team about what is technologically possible. Both about the development in hand at the moment and about development for future work. Product Managers need to reconcile what the technology can do with what customers need. The advancing nature of technology means there is an ever-increasing set of opportunities that earlier technology could not address.

Consequently, Product Managers need to stay abreast of technology developments. Product Managers should see the technical delivery team as a source of insights. They work with technology every day and can often see possibilities early.

It also means that Product Managers need to be in an ongoing dialogue with customers. Both customers who have already bought the product and are using it, and potential customers, the kind of customers the company wants to have.

The Market

Product Managers rarely create products for single customers. Contrast this with Business Analysts who frequently find themselves creating a product for one customer. Product Managers create products for a market or market segment. Segmenting the market allows for different products to target to different segments.

Market segmentation is an important consideration for Product Managers. Slight product modifications for different segments can make similar products more successful. Equally, commercially challenging segments might be best avoided.

While customers should be to the fore in the examination of any market, Product Managers need to look more broadly. There will always be competitors in any market. Product Managers need to know who the competitors are and keep a watch on them. They need to attend trade shows and read trade journals, watch competitors' web sites, and talk to customers of competitors.

Product Managers sometimes become too obsessed with competitors. They want to match competitors feature for feature. Rather than focusing on customers and helping customers, they focus on competing with rivals. Companies who adopt fast-follower strategies—like Rocket Internet in Germany—may well be justified in obsessing about competitors. Usually such obsession is a bad sign.

To some degree Product Managers can choose their customer by defining their segment. In doing so they can define who their competitors are. In *Crossing the Chasm*, Geoffrey Moore suggests defining a market so that your product is superior to your chosen competitors. By doing this, products which customers might consider superior to yours get defined away as competitors.

TEXT PROCESSING SEGMENTATION

Consider the market for text processing. While Microsoft Word dominates the market, there are specialist products in different segments. Legal offices and Government offices continue to use Word Perfect because it caters for these customers particularly well. Apple customers may use Pages rather than Word. When I blog, I use a program called MacJournal which is actually targeted at those keeping a diary. But I am writing this text with a program called iAWriter which I find great for my needs. Many professional writers prefer Scrivener. Then there is EverNote... I could continue naming text processing applications.

On first sight Microsoft Word dominates the market for text processing. But within that market, there are hundreds of segments where other companies can make a living. Looked at one way, this is one large market with lots of niches. Looked at another way, this is many different markets with similar characteristics.

By one definition MacJournal, BlogJet, and other blogging applications compete with Microsoft Word in the writing and text processing market. For most writing needs, these applications are far inferior to Word, they have limited spelling and grammar checking, they lack most formatting options, and have no equation editor. But when it comes to posting a blog, it is Word which lacks capabilities.

Senior managers and strategy

One popular definition of a Product Manager is "the CEO of the Product." Certainly, in a small one-product company, the Product Manager may well be the CEO. But by the time a company gets large enough to have multiple dedicated Product Managers, there is usually a dedicated CEO too. While a Product Manager may well see themselves as CEO of the Product, there is an actual CEO—and other senior managers—to work with.

Some of this work will be mundane: Product Mangers may well need to report sales and product plans, provide updates on team changes, and more. As much as they shouldn't need to, Product Managers are likely to find themselves making the case for more resources. How much mundane work they take on may well depend on what other specialists are available.

Product Managers will also need to share some of their findings on customers and markets with more senior managers who will, in turn, share their own findings. Again, this is a two-way conversation.

Product Managers need to know what senior managers are attempting to do. They need to understand company strategy, and they need to work to ensure their product strategy is aligned with company strategy. Product Mangers will also influence corporate strategy thought their findings and the strategy for their product.

Sales

There are even more tasks that fall to Product Managers which are not shown in the earlier diagram and are not core to the role. Such tasks vary from place to place, but one non-core activity deserves mentioning: sales support.

The need to assist with sales is greater for Product Managers working in business to business (B2B) or enterprise software fields. Those working on business to customer (B2C) products are less likely to get involved in individual sales. In these cases, Product Managers may want to inject themselves into the sales process to hear the voice of the customer themselves.

There can be few, if any, B2B Product Managers who are not on occasions called in by sales staff to help with a customer account. Most Product Managers do more sales support than they like but eliminating it completely would remove a valuable source of information.

Sometimes Product Managers need to go out with sales staff and listen to customers. Being a fly on the wall can provide useful insights to the Product Manager. Appearing in person with the salesperson add weight to a bid.

Sometimes they need to present to customers and help make the case that the product has a bright future. Sometimes they may even need to make the commercial pitch themselves.

And sometimes they may need to promise particular features to land a big sale. I wish it wasn't so, but it usually is. On the whole Product Manager should avoid promising specific features as a sweetener to getting a deal signed. It may close one deal, but it stores up problems. When it becomes routine practice, market focus and development schedules suffer. This is especially so when features get promised for specific dates.

For these reasons Product Managers should shy away from presenting product roadmaps with dates and promises. Roadmaps, if they exist at all, should describe possible futures—they are scenario plans. And they change.

Product Managers need to engage with sales because they need to have credibility with sales. These same Product Managers will sometimes need to tell sales people that they will not, cannot, make a product modification to close one sale. Product Managers who become "Dr. No" are unlikely to last long in the company.

When engaging with sales staff and individual customers, Product Managers need to remember that the sales person is dealing with one sale and the customer in front of them is one customer.

Product Managers are concerned with markets: the aggregation of customers. Sales staff deal with one customer at a time.

Changes in Product Management

Once upon a time, product management was part of the secret source of Silicon Valley. Product management hid in open site, but the rest of the world was slow to catch on.

In the last 10–15 years, the rest of the world has noticed. Product management is now found all over the world. By most standards it is still a young profession, but it has matured and grown rapidly as it has spread. It has also changed rapidly.

The profession itself has found better ways of working, but many of the changes have been driven from outside the profession. The rise of agile development has been something of a double-edged sword. On the plus side, it highlights the importance of the product focus through the Product Owner role. However, by using the title "Product Owner," agile has sowed confusion and endless debate.

Perhaps more importantly the increasing power of our machines—ubiquitous cheap CPU cycles—has created tools which reshape the role and open possibilities yesterday's Product Manager could only dream of.

© Allan Kelly 2019

A. Kelly, *The Art of Agile Product Ownership*,

https://doi.org/10.1007/978-1-4842-5168-3_16

This new generation of tools makes it easier for Product Managers to do their job without leaving their desk. Instrumentation and recording tools provide Product Managers with insights into customer behavior without the need to actually meet customers.

On a technical level, more powerful tools, and changes in development such as continual delivery and DevOps, mean it can often be quick to build something and see how customers react. Lengthy research and analysis can be replaced by building a small product, making it available to customers and seeing what happens. Not only can this approach be faster, it can be more accurate because one is looking at what customers do, not what customer say they will do. Consequently, Product Managers can take a more experimental approach to their role—sometimes called hypothesis-driven development.

Still more profound at the strategic level, increased computing power is driving the digitization of business—or perhaps more accurately the *softwarization* of business. No longer is software development confined to dedicated software companies. Universally present, all ways on internet connectivity, available on computers, tablets, phones, televisions, watches, and elsewhere means every business is potentially a digital business.

The prototypes of digital business are the previous generation of Internet companies: SalesForce, Google, and Facebook. These companies themselves followed the patterns of Microsoft, Oracle, IBM, Borland, and countless others. These companies developed the role of the Product Manager.

Now that every company is a digital company, every business is dependent on software technology—the need for Product Managers, Product Management skills, and expertise is greater than ever.

Just do it

Cheap and plentiful CPU cycles have driven massive changes in how software is created. Improvements in development tools and commodity cloud infrastructure mean that creating products—especially minimal products—is an order of magnitude cheaper than it was.

At the time of the dot.com boom, building a web application would take weeks at least. Therefore, there was great incentive to make sure the right thing was being built. Today, advances in development tools—languages like Ruby and JavaScript—and commoditized hosting—servers for rent by the second from Amazon plus application containerization with tools like Docker—mean it is far quicker and cheaper to build a product.

As a result, it can be quicker to build something and see how the market reacts than it is to formulate an understanding of how the market might react. Factoring in the cost of delay incurred while researching a product and the case for starting development immediately becomes compelling.

Techniques such as A/B testing and multi-variance testing allow similar approaches for existing applications. This allows decisions over what to build to be deferred until later. Equally, improvements in development tools and processes mean that once a decision gets made, the delivery should take far less time.

New research approaches

Tools for tracking user activities have leapt ahead. Not only does the ability to track user actions save Product Managers time, but it can also improve their understanding of users.

While some desktop applications were programmed to report user activities, few companies did this. Even fewer actually reported the data or acted upon it. Applications with web interfaces lend themselves to annotation and tracking.

For example, Google Analytics allows Product Managers to see which pages customers visit. From this they can infer what interests customers. Other tools can track user actions in more detail and allow more inferences.

Taking this further, there now exist web sites that allow Product Managers to solicit user experience. UserTesting.com is one of these. For a fee, Product Managers can select a demographic group of interest, say stay-at-home mothers, and ask that people meeting this profile try their software.

In return, the Product Manager will receive a transcript of the actions undertaken by the sample users. They may receive a voice recording of the subject talking through their experience and even a screen recording showing the screen and mouse movements.

Such tools are valuable to both Product Managers and interface designers. Using such tools, a larger user sample can be gathered in less time and with less travel.

Lean start-up

Eric Ries' book *The Lean Startup*[1] is the usual reference for those advocating a "build something and track the market reaction"—or build-measure-learn as it is more generally called—rather than the "work out everything in advance" approach. The book is a very engaging read and explains how Ries deployed these techniques in his own company and elsewhere.

---

[1] Eric Ries, *The Lean Startup* (Crown Publishing Group, 2011).

Ries' mentor was Steve Blank. His book *The Four Steps to the Epiphany* sets out a structured approach to product and market discovery. Blank calls for a Customer Development team rather than a Product Manager in start-ups:

> The job of the Customer Development team is to see whether there are customers and a market for that vision.[2]

Both books should be required reading for Product Managers and Product Owners. (consequently I will not repeat the arguments here.)

More formally the "build something and see what happens" approach gets called "Hypothesis-Driven Development" or "Build, Measure, Learn." Advocates reference the scientific model which many readers will recall from school:

- Formulate a hypothesis about what will happen.

- Devise an experiment to prove, or disprove, the hypothesis.

- Perform the experiment and examine the result to determine whether the hypothesis holds.

For example, one might hypothesize that the company web site will make more sales if it contains more pictures of products. As an experiment traffic to the site gets divided into two groups: A and B for a week. Group A see the existing web site, while Group B see a version with more product pictures. At the end of the week, the sales statistics for each group will show which made the most sales. The version making the most money gets kept.

The result here may seem obvious but it illustrates the point. There are companies that work exactly like this; Amazon is a frequently cited example.

Those who have studied science at a more advanced level may recall that the scientific method contains one earlier step: literature review.

Before formulation, the hypothesis investigators will review what is already known in a field. They may repeat the review after formulating a hypothesis to see if an experiment is necessary. In the preceding case, one might well find existing evidence that customers spend more money when shown pictures of products.

A review of existing knowledge should be an essential step in any scientific approach. However, an exhaustive review would return to the pre-agile days of long documents and decisions based on analysis alone. As is so often the case, the right approach is somewhere in the middle.

---

[2] Steve Blank, *The Four Steps to Epiphany* (K&S Ranch, 2013).

Product Managers need to both stay up to date with the latest thinking in the field. Intuition can, and should, guide when to create an experiment. They should be a little more skeptical of their intuition than they have been before, and a little more prepared to try experiments a bit more often—even if they fail.

Quantitative vs. Qualitative

As amazing as many of these developments are, it is still important—perhaps more important—for Product Managers to actually meet customers and potential customers. This is because technology can tell us what a customer does, but it cannot tell us what they are thinking, feeling, nor explain the customer's intention.

Most of these technology advances can only provide quantitative data, for example, 50 out of 60 users clicked the help button. Technology cannot—yet—provide qualitative data: *What was the customer thinking when they did that?*

It is not enough to understand the numbers. In order to know what numbers to look at, and what to track, there needs to be some understanding of both customer and product.

Faced with more tools and more data than ever before about what customers are doing, there is a danger of both overload and misplaced confidence. First, the influx of data creates a lot more material to analyze—more pressure on time.

Second, the same data can make a Product Manager feel they understand the customer. But qualitative data alone can never explain what customers are thinking. Qualitative research complements quantitative data.

Internal analysis

The change towards software as a service means there is a greater need for Product Managers to pay attention to the business processes within their organization. It is no use having a brilliant product if the organization makes it hard for customers to access the product or places unnecessary restrictions on use.

When software products get delivered as a service, the service needs considering in its entirety. The customer journey from the first contact to job done is the unit of analysis. When software shipped on a CD, each buyer created their own services—and processes—around the software product. When software sells as a service, the vendor exerts far more influence over how to use the service and the business processes around it.

As a result, Product Managers need to sometimes think like a Business Analyst, both about their own organization and the customer organizations. Within the vendor, Product Managers need to consider how to support the service and how the organization works with customers. Meanwhile, to realize the full benefits of a software service buyers may need to update their own business processes.

Design to the forefront

Product Managers have always needed to consider product design. But product design has often been an afterthought - or even overlooked entirely. Consequently, Product Managers were often the designer of last resort.

The success of Apple in recent years demonstrates the need to make product design a first-class consideration. Technically the iPhone does little that Android does not. Yet Apple design allows the iPhone to command higher pricing and has made Apple one of the most valuable companies.

At the same time, the world of design has moved forward. User experience design (UXD) has replaced mere interface design. The best designers are combined great design skills with user research and analysis skills that complement Product Managers.

Today's product designers are an essential partner to Product Managers in deciding not just what the product does but how the product does it.

The Business Analyst Role

An internal consultancy role that has the responsibility for investigating business systems, identifying options for improving business systems and bridging the needs of the business with the use of IT.

—Debra Paul and Donald Yates[1]

The Product Owner role is frequently staffed by a Business Analyst (BA). This can make a lot of sense. The core of both roles is understanding what is needed and communicating this to a development team. Many of the skills required by Product Owners are exactly the skills Business Analysts are trained and experienced in using: stakeholder identification and management, requirements analysis, specification, communication, evaluation, etc.

Some dislike this approach. There are those who will argue—with good reason—that the Product Owner should not be a proxy. The Product Owner should be someone who has a vested interest in the product and really wants it to succeed. However, this "Ideal Product Owner" is not always possible:

---

[1] Debra Paul and Donald Yates, eds., *Business Analysis* (The British Computer Society, 2006).

© Allan Kelly 2019
A. Kelly, *The Art of Agile Product Ownership*,
https://doi.org/10.1007/978-1-4842-5168-3_17

Sometimes there are many different people who can legitimately claim the Product Owner role. Casting anyone as the "one true Product Owner" would not be fair to the other and the interests they represent.

Sometimes the right person to be Product Owner is just not available; they have too many other demands on them.

In many cases when the right person is not available, the best thing to do would be to cancel the work altogether. Far too often key stakeholders are not prepared, or not able, to invest the time and energy required. This itself is a warning sign and continuing may simply build up problems for later.

On other occasion the best answer is to appoint a Product Owner proxy. Such a person needs the skills to do the role and the trust of the ultimate Product Owner(s). Specifically, they need: authority to decide what needs to be done, legitimacy to do the role, and the time to do the work properly.

In many ways Business Analysts are professional proxies and sometimes that is exactly what is needed in a Product Owner. On other occasions proxies lack power and authority to get work done.

Nor are BAs destined to play the Product Owner every time. In fact, there is a whole host of ways in which a professional BA can help a delivery team.

The skills of a BA can be very useful in assisting a Product Owner who has never had to work with delivery teams and other stakeholders. The analysis skills of a BA can help the rest of the team understand problems and create solutions.

It is worth taking a step back and looking at the Business Analyst role in more depth.

Business Analyst or Product Manager?

Business Analysts are close cousins of Product Managers, and like Product Managers, they are concerned with "what should the software do in order to maximize the return on investment." The mindset is similar as are many of the tools. But there is a big difference.

A Business Analyst is concerned with analyzing a business problem or a business process (Figure 17-1). They are looking to improve things within one organization. They are less concerned with the market than with internal constraints.

Figure 17-1. Business Analysts look at stakeholders and users inside the corporation

The natural home of a Business Analyst (BA) is inside a corporation, such as Unilever, HSBC, Chrysler, Glaxo-Smith-Kline, and so on. The BA has more users, not customers, and those users are usually captive. If a Product Manager introduces a bad application, customers will not buy it; if a BA introduces a bad product, then users have little choice but to use it.

I always imagine the natural home of the BA is one of those skyscrapers in Canary Wharf or Manhattan. For the BA almost everyone they need to speak to is in that building. A BA can ride up and down in the elevator to meet everyone they need to.

This is in stark contrast to the Product Manager role. A Product Manager's customers are almost certainly not in the same building (Figure 17-2). One of the first tasks facing any Product Manager is to identify who their customers are or who should be customers. Meeting customer can be a challenge when they are on the other side of the world.

Corporations often staff the Product Owner role with a BA. This can work very well because BAs are, by training, customer proxies. But sometimes BAs lack the authority to make real decisions and end up being little more than order takers.

Figure 17-2. Product Managers look at (potential) customers outside the organization

Analysis

In the IT context, a BA is someone concerned with information systems for business applications.[2] Thus, the role is IT centric but extends beyond the pure technology system to include the processes and practices of people who use the system.

BAs are concerned with the analysis of systems, processes, practices, and operations within an organization. They are tasked with understanding these things and proposing changes. But they are not tasked with designing those changes in detail.

BAs often find their role extends beyond the system and becomes change management. This is natural because a technology system forms part of a large system, a system that includes people. Changing one part of the technology has a knock-on effect.

In understanding these systems and suggesting changes, the BA is expected to take into account the overall business objectives and direction. It is unlikely the BA will have responsibility for revenue or cost saving, but they may be called on to provide financial analysis.

---

[2] As we'll discuss in Chapter 18, there are other Business Analysts who are not concerned with technology systems.

Business Analysis maturity model

Debra Paul of Assist KD has suggested a business analysis maturity model.[3] In this model the scope of the BA role increases as the authority of the BA increases. See Figure 17-3.

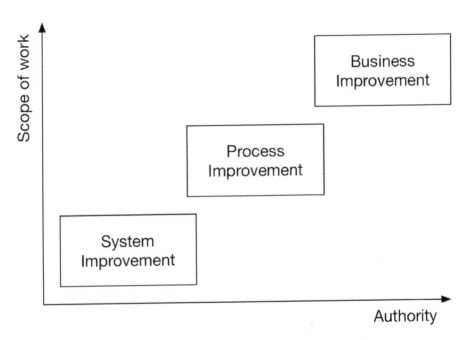

Figure 17-3. Business Analysis maturity model

Viewed from an individual perspective, a newly graduated business analyst may find that their authority and the scope of their work are both constrained— bottom-left corner. Such BAs are often seen as order takers; they visit stakeholders, ask them what they would like the new system to do, write it down, and move onto the next stakeholder.

Like a restaurant waiter, while they be asked their recommendation or suggest choices, final decision authority rests elsewhere. Their success is often measured by the successful delivery of requested orders.

As the BAs' authority grows, the scope of their work increases. Rather than simply write down what other people want of a system, they are able to

---

[3] Paul has outlined the BA maturity model in many presentations and discussed it with the author. The model is described on the Assist KD web site, www.assistkd.com/knowledge-hub/business-analysis-maturity-model.

consider the wider context. Using their analysis skills, they are able to advise on, and even suggest, improvements to the processes.

With more authority a BA can look even wider and consider the business not just the process. Now their role is one of finding business improvements—which might just be realized by IT enhancements.

The beauty of this model is that is applies not just to individual BAs as their career advances but to the organization as a whole. Many organizations have an immature view of the BA role. For them a BA is a bridge between "real users" and the "geeks" who create technology. The BA is expected to translate business need to gobbledegook for techies and back again. As such they are not expected to suggest process changes, let alone business.

Yet this approach is a waste of time and resources. If a BA is there to just write documents and pass messages from one side to another side, the role is probably worth eliminating. The development team can talk directly to stakeholders and demonstrate enhanced products themselves.

As Adrian Reed[4] has pointed out, the bridge model could be applied to family doctors: their role is to act as a bridge between the customer (ill person) and pharmacist (who speaks complex medical language).

More mature organization recognize that BAs—like doctors—have a range of skills which can add value far above that of order taker. Such organizes use BAs as trusted consultants to advice on how the company as a whole can improve.

Discovery

Both Product Manager and BA roles traditionally center on requirements discovery, that is, enquiring and analyzing the application domain to uncover the requirements of a technology system to improve the domain.

Perhaps the biggest change agile software development creates for Business Analysts is that of timing. In traditional development a BA would do most of their work before any code was cut. A BA may even disengage before programming began. In an agile environment, discovery and refinement is an ongoing activity. Rather than all requirements being determined in advance (a big batch), they are determined on a just-in-time basis.

This means the work of a BA will change from day to day. Some days the BA role is one of collecting business needs in order to analyze the needs and communicate them to those responsible for technology solutions. The next day they may be working with a Programmer or Testers to deliver those fresh

---

[4] Adrian Reed, "It's Time to Ditch the Bridge," 21 April 2016, www.adrianreed.co.uk/2016/04/21/its-time-to-ditch-the-bridge/.

requirements. On other occasions the same BA may act as an internal consultant, helping the business understand what is possible and envisaging a different way of working by using technology.

BA or PO?

According to Debra Paul and Donald Yates:

Although there are different role definitions, depending on the organization, there does seem to be an area of common ground where most Business Analysts work. ...

- *To investigate business systems ...*

- *To identify actions required to improve the operation of the business*

- *To document the business requirements for the IT system*[5]

Given the variety of work expected of BAs, finding a definition of the role is problematic. A definition becomes harder still when one tries to define the BA roles as distinct from the Product Owner role.

A Business Analyst who finds themselves working on an agile team should not ask: "What is the BA role on an agile team?"

Rather they should ask: "How can a BA, with the skills and experience that a BA brings, help this team perform as best it can?"

If the team lacks a Product Owner, then the BA may well throw themselves into that role. If the team has a Product Owner who is struggling with the role—perhaps because they lack experience—then the BA may well be the ideal person to help.

But there are a myriad of ways someone with business analysis skills; training and experience can help an agile delivery team. It just depends on what the team actually needs.

---

[5] Debra Paul and Donald Yates, eds., *Business Analysis* (The British Computer Society, 2006).

Different Types of Business Analysts

While the Product Manager role is often overlooked, the Business Analyst (BA) role is often misunderstood. This is because under the title of Business Analyst, there are many different types of BA. Some of these roles carry the BA title erroneously; things would be simplified if some BAs were given the title "Assistant Product Manager."

There is debate within the BA community itself as to the proper role for analysts. Therefore, it is important not to look on the role either too narrowly or to assume that all BAs work the same way. At the same time, some of those who have the job title Business Analyst might more accurately reflect the role individuals perform.

Non-IT

There are Business Analysts who have nothing to do with IT. They may use the same tools and skillsets as a technology BA may draw on additional tools too. But they don't do it in order to create or change IT systems.

© Allan Kelly 2019
A. Kelly, *The Art of Agile Product Ownership*,
https://doi.org/10.1007/978-1-4842-5168-3_18

For example, some Business Analysts are engaged in market analysis. They work for asset managers and the like. They analyze businesses, business trends, markets, competitors, and anything else that is connected with commerce and helps their employer.

There is nothing wrong with this type of BA; it is just necessary to point out that not everyone with the title Business Analyst is concerned with IT systems.

As business becomes increasingly digital, as more and more business processes and activities become embedded in software, more and more of these analysts will find they need to consider technology in one form or another.

Systems Analyst

Before Business Analysts became a common in IT departments, it was normal to find Systems Analysts. These analysts perform a similar function—deciding what should be in the system and what should not—but they focused on the computer system not the business. (Some Business Analysts are formally titled as Business Systems Analyst.)

This type of analysis creates a technology focus for work rather than a business focus. For example:

> "What can the computer system do to improve the payroll process?" as opposed to "How can we improve the payroll process, possibly using a computer system?"

Asking "what might the system do" probably made sense when the use of computers in business was new, when CPU cycles were expensive, and computers had only a fraction of today's power. Back then people and companies needed to explore what might be done.

Today things are different. With the massive power of today's computers, one might assume "the computer can do anything." Understanding the business need comes to the fore.

Although, sometimes, particularly with new technology, it can be worthwhile asking "what might this wonderful technology be capable of?" Possibly, artificial intelligence is going through that phase right now.

But **Business Analysis is not System Analysis.** If a company really needs a System Analyst, then they should appoint one.

The origins of the Business Analyst role are in the System Analyst role. But over the years, the business analysis aspects of systems analysis have grown into a distinct role itself. Similarly, the technical aspects of systems analysis grew into the software architect role. In many cases this role itself has been superseded as design has devolved to the programming team as a whole.

As with Business Analysts, there is a group of Systems Analysts who have little or nothing to do with technology systems. Their role is to analyze and advice on other "systems." For example, a production line is a system, and a system analyst might work on improving the manufacturing process.

Technical BAs

Some BAs, and Systems Analysts, actually take a role in designing software. While many BAs become involved—rightly or wrongly—with designing the user interface, these BAs are concerned with the internal, almost code level, software design. Such people sometimes get called *Technical Business Analysts* but not always. Whether they have the word *technical* in their official title or not, I consider BAs who get involved with internal software design *Technical Business Analysts*.

To my mind this is a misuse of the BA role. BAs are primarily concerned with analysis; creating software is synthesis. The roles are different. BAs should focus on the business; software design should be left to the specialists.

This is not to exclude BAs from design conversations; they can provide an excellent sounding board to more technical people. But usually BAs do not have the extensive software design skill of Programmers and software architects. And if a BA does have such extensive skills, one wonders whether they might be better suited to working on that side of the equation.

In asking analysts to design, "the business" may believe it is more likely to get what it wants from development teams. Yet the net effect is to move some of the design activity from those who are best placed to do it to those who are less able.

BAs should not design software. BAs should confine their role to analysis and determining what the business needs from the software and systems.

By concentrating on the business need, the BA provides the team with room to create a solution. The more a BA specifies system constraints, or design details, the greater the restriction on the team. When this happens, requirements contain design constraints.

Personally, I view Business Analysts who engage in software design as a historical quirk. These analysts have retained that part of the System Analyst role which concerned itself with system design.

Business Analyst as Product Manager

In some companies Product Managers exist; they fulfil the type of external analysis described in other chapters, but they bear the title Business Analyst. This may be because the company has its origins in corporate IT—perhaps it was spun out of a corporate IT department. Or perhaps the company does not understand the Product Manager role. This used to be fairly common in the United Kingdom when the Product Manager role was little known.

Whatever the reason, the fact is: some BAs are Product Managers with incorrect titles.

Occasionally companies have both Product Managers and Business Analysts. Usually the BA is not really filling a BA role, they are a Junior Product Manager, or they are a System Analyst.

As we noted before there is a lot of work for a Product Manager to do. One way of reducing the work load is to appoint specialists to help them in some way. In these cases, a BA works as an assistant to the Product Manager on some specific aspect of the product.

Sometimes the BA provides the detail. While Product Manager concerns themselves with market and customers, a BA may concern themselves with the detail of what is being asked for. In effect the BA is working to support this team in filling the request of the Product Manager. This is particularly true when BA is a subject matter expert.

For example, a BA may pick up the competitor monitoring work from the Product Manager. The BA will be able to spend more time monitoring, investigating, and analyzing the competition and then feed this information to the Product Manager. Such BAs would more accurately be called Assistant Product Managers—although such a title might imply a subservient role so is probably best avoided.

Subject Matter Expert

It is possible to work in IT and yet know little about the application domain under development. For example, a Java developer may use their knowledge of Java programming for a bank, or an oil company, or for a telecoms company. While it helps to have domain knowledge, it is not always essential to start with. Skills like Java programming are transferable.

Complex domains need individuals who have in-depth understanding. For example, banks need banking experts and telecoms companies need communication experts. For these individuals, skills such as coding are secondary to their knowledge of the domain. Such people are often known as Subject Matter Experts.

Again, some of those with the title Business Analyst are actually something else: some BAs are Subject Matter Experts; their knowledge is more important in understanding what needs to be done than analysis.

Since the Business Analyst role entails understanding and describing organizations and technical domains, Subject Matter Experts (SMEs) may gravitate to this title.

Yet it is not a foregone conclusion that a BA needs to be an expert in the domain to perform their role. Indeed, being an expert in current practices may blind one to opportunities for change. Starting an analysis assignment with an open mind, or blank sheet of paper, may be advantageous.

BA as support

There are many other ways in which a BA can bring their skills and knowledge to support a development without taking on the Product Owner role:

A BA may help a Product Owner in numerous ways:

- Taking on analysis and research to give the PO more time

- Helping a new PO to understand how to fill their role, sharing their skills in requirements gathering, communication, forecasting, etc.

- Deputizing for a PO when they are visiting customers

- Acting as a channel for stakeholders outside the team to make share their own needs

A BA may work with Programmers and Testers too:

- Using the BA's knowledge of the business to write acceptance criteria and tests; perhaps taking part in "3-Amigos" sessions or pairing with a developer as they practice BDD

- Using analysis skills to dissect problems and search for solutions

- Undertake user research with, or instead of, development team members

- Act as an extra pair of hands in exploratory testing, documentation and, support request

In particular BA can bring their analysis skills to bear on the team itself. Because BAs look at entire systems, they frequently see ways in which the delivery team, which is a system itself, can work better and improve. The facilitation skills many BAs have help here.

Similarly, BAs can make very effective Scrum Masters and Agile Coaches because of their facilitation skills and end-to-end view point.

Many hats

BAs can and do wear multiple hats—sometimes at the same time!

While it may add to confusion, it is a tribute to the flexibility of the BA skillset that professional BAs can get called upon to fill a number of different jobs all under the one job title. An individual BA on one project work as an internal consultant to help invent a solution. The next project may be somewhat simpler and only need the BA to capture requirements. Later in the same project, the same BA may take on the Scrum Master role or help with the testing of the final software.

The core BA skill is analysis: the ability to analyze, to understand a domain and a problem, then to communicate what needs to be done to change it.

Some BAs bring a wealth of domain experience. Such knowledge can be very useful but so too can a fresh pair of eyes and a different perspective.

I am sometimes heard to say: the secret of the Business Analyst's role is in the name—Business, Analyst. Some BAs are fantastic BAs because they are great analysts. Other BAs are great at their job because they understand the business in depth and have specialist knowledge.

Product Owner or junior Product Manager?

I regularly meet people who are designated Product Owners but who play a supporting role to a Product Manager. Such Product Owners may even have a reporting line to the Product Manager. Usually these Product Owners are little more than Backlog Administrators for a Product Manager who is too busy to work with the team.

This is absolutely crazy. Think about it for one minute.

Who are the most important people in your organization? Who command ultimate authority? Who takes the profit?

In most commercial organizations, it is the Owners, the shareholders, the people who legally have the authority to sell or close the company.

Managers are hired help. Owners employ managers.

It is crazy to make *Owners* junior to *Managers*.

There is one industry where Owners do see less of the profits than the Managers: banking. Banks regularly reward top managers with handsome bonuses, while shareholders have to make do with meager and reduced dividends.

Perhaps that's why so many Product Owners who report to Product Managers seem to work in banking.

Customer and Subject Matter Expert

Extreme Programming[1] defines a similar role called the customer. Indeed, many have interpreted XP's customer role to mean an actual customer. For the original XP team—the Chrysler Comprehensive Compensation team—the customer was a subject matter expert, someone steeped in how the current system worked and highly knowledgeable about the domain the team are working in.

Such experts are frequently referred to as Subject Matter Experts (SMEs), or Domain Experts. In complex fields SMEs can be essential in helping the team understand what is to be built. However, such experts can also be a indrance, because of their expert knowledge in the *as is* they may not see the possibility for how things could be.

Recruiting such experts to the team is an example of the *Poacher Turned Game Keeper Pattern*.[2] While it is entirely possible on some endeavors to have an actual customer—or user—join the team and fill this role, it is not always possible.

This is especially true when a team is created a mass-market product. For example, if the Microsoft Word team were to employ a customer, which customer would they employ? Would they choose someone representative of their North American customers? Or their Chinese customers? Someone from an office environment? Or a student?

Had the Microsoft team recruited a typical user of Word in the early days of the product, they may have employed a former secretary accustomed to taking dictation and transcribing a letter. Yet this is a role that Word—and other office automation tools—has almost eliminated.

One of my own clients creates software that is used on sea going vessels. A typical customer for them is an experienced ship's officer. While such people sometimes come onshore to work, I know from personal experience they can be unhappy in land-based manufacturing or office environment. Getting an actual customer - or even just user - to work with a team can be difficult.

The other problem with hiring an actual customer is that such people have a half-life: they are valuable for the team because of their specialist know-how. The longer the work with the team the more their customer knowledge becomes dated.

Finally, hiring an actual customer may have a sting in the tail: the person with the expertise who is keenest to work with the team might well be the team's greatest supporter in the client space. Removing such a person from the work

---

[1] K. Beck, *Extreme Programming Explained* (Addison-Wesley, 2000).
[2] A. Kelly, *Business Patterns for Software Developers* (Chichester: John Wiley & Sons, 2012).

itself may reduce traction with those using the product, and this can be a significant problem for commercial software sellers.

Project Manager

Notice that so far, no mention has been made of the Project Manager role. There is a good reason for this, and it is the same reason why the Product Owner role is not a Project Manage role—although unfortunately too many organizations erroneously conflate the two roles.

Recall the Project Manager's iron triangle, Figure 1-1 in Chapter 1. Traditional Project Managers are largely trained to deliver a defined thing: a statement of work, a bill of materials, a set of requirements. The assumption in much project management is that the right thing to do and deliver has already been defined. The role of the Project Manager is to deliver the thing within the constraints of time, cost, resources, and quality.

However, the roles described in this chapter all deal with defining the thing to be built. Business Analysts define the thing to be built by looking inside the business; Product Managers define the thing to be built by looking at the market and potential customer needs; and Subject Matter Experts define the thing to be built using their expert knowledge.

In some domains the thing can be defined, and project management skills can be used to deliver it as requested. However, in much knowledge work, and particularly in software development, the thing to be built is at best in a state of flux and at worst totally unknown.

This is not to say the skills of Project Managers and Project Manager training is not useful to Product Owners, it can be, but the Product Owner role is fundamentally different because product ownership—and agile methods in general—work by varying the thing Project Managers seek to keep constant.

Other role models

Product Managers and Business Analyst (BA) are the most common—and therefore most important—role models for Product Owners, but they are not the only ones.

Sometimes organizations appoint Product Champions. I can't say I'm sure what a Product Champion actually does. I imagine him or her evangelizing the product to customers and internal stakeholders. Certainly, a Product Owner may need to do some of this.

In some environments Business Analysts are expected to be detail oriented, and the bigger questions are left to a Business Partner role. This split has similarities to the Strategic Product Owner/Tactical Product Owner model which will be discussed later.

Some organizations still have the Systems Analyst (SA) role. This role has largely disappeared as servers and PCs have replaced mainframes but some SAs still exist. The role can look somewhat confusing because it operates on both the supply and demand sides.

On the one side, SAs play a part in the design of software—and even computer—systems (as mentioned above when discussing Technical Business Analysts). This harks back to the days when knowing whether a computer could do something was a far bigger issue. Today senior developers and architects pick up most such work.

On the other side, SAs are concerned with "what should the system do." The rise of the BA has supplanted the SA here as BAs normally (should) take a more commercial view on what should be done.

Where do Product Owners come from?

Product Owners can come from the demand side: they may be experts in what is needed because they are the people who need it. Such people may have no previous experience working with technology teams, but this does not invalidate their right to hold the role. It does however make it more complicated; they may need assistance—possibly from a Business Analyst or deputy Product Owner—to fulfil the role.

Product Owners can also come from the supply side - it is not uncommon to find a former Programmer filling the PO role. Product Owners are a type of requirements engineer who works within an (agile) team. Some will be "heavyweight" requirements engineer steeped in requirements engineering tools and processes. Most likely they will come from a Business Analyst's or Product Manager's background and arrive ready to use their existing toolkit.

There is no right or wrong place for Product Owners to come from.

Challenges

I believe the Product Owner role is the hardest role to fill well on a team. At the same time, I believe it is the single most important role on a team. I know others who have seen the role up close and agree with me. Unfortunately, from a distance, this challenge is not always clear.

Although the Product Owner role builds on earlier roles and skillsets, it is itself a new role. Sure, Scrum introduced the role nearly 20 years ago, but until recently it has only been found in a minority of companies.

That means: almost nobody has held the title "Product Owner" for more than 20 years. Nobody has been appointed POs for more than 20 years. Nobody has been managing POs for more than 20 years. In fact, in most organizations leaders and managers have far less than 20 years of experience with Product Owners—or indeed Scrum and agile. Consequently, almost everybody, senior and junior alike, are still learning about the role and what to expect from Product Owners.

As more companies utilize Product Owners, and as more individuals fill the role, more people will come to understand the benefits a good PO can bring, and the challenges all POs face.

In closing this book, I want to look at some of those challenges. Awareness is the first step to resolving them. But it is not all challenge and gloom.

There are solutions out there. As the role—and indeed agile—is still in its early stages, one hopes to see a lot of experimentation. Individuals and teams need to address these challenges and let successful patterns emerge.

I describe one such model—the SPO/TPO split—in the next chapter. This pattern appears again and again in organizations even if the titles used in the two roles differ.

Although let me single out one pet hate here. Too often I see Strategic Product Owners called "Product Managers," while Tactical Product Owners get called "Product Owners." Normally I don't much care what titles get used for the SPO and TPO roles, but this arrangement annoys me.

In this arrangement the SPO "Product Manager" is frequently seen as superior to the TPO "Product Owner." To repeat what I stated in the previous chapter: ask yourself, who are the most important people in an organization?

It is not a manager of any sort. Managers are little more than hired help.

The most important people in any organization[1] are the owners. Maybe owners of shares traded on a stock market, maybe private equity investors, or maybe the original founders. In any organizational hierarchy the owners are at the very top.

In the real world, managers report to owners. So surely Product Managers should report to Product Owners?

---

[1] This is not to belittle the legitimate claims of customers, employees, society, and other stakeholders; rather this statement is a reflection on the typical corporate paradigm.

The Product Owner Refactored

Perhaps in the ideal world, the Product Owner would not exist. The team would contain a mix of business and customer facing skills together with technology knowledge and would work together to produce the right thing.

Indeed, this model sometimes exists in teams of one—which really isn't a team. From time to time individuals possess both the technical skills to create a software product and to understand what is needed. Such individuals can create great products. Being in the right place at the right time helps too, as when experienced Programmer Dan Bricklin saw an opportunity and created the first electronic spreadsheet, VisiCalc, in 1979.

But this model has, at least, two distinct problems: it relies on luck and, even more problematic, is difficult to scale.

So, the Product Owner (Figure 19-1). Having a designated, and skilled, Product Owner can be a great step forward for many teams. Where a team has to decide between many requests from different customers having someone in the middle can be a major step forward.

© Allan Kelly 2019
A. Kelly, *The Art of Agile Product Ownership*,
https://doi.org/10.1007/978-1-4842-5168-3_19

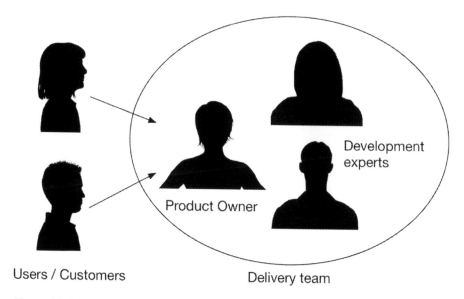

Users / Customers   Delivery team

Figure 19-1. Product Owner is the team member specializing in customer requests and needs

A team can get a lot of mileage from this Product Owner—especially when, as described in other chapters here, the Product Owner is supported by the team and other specialists. However, as a team grows, and as more products are added to a portfolio, this model too has scaling problems.

One solution is to split the role in two with one Product Owner taking a Strategic view and another a Tactical view.

Strategic and Tactical Product Owners

When deciding what to work on, POs need to consider a wide range of factors and draw on many sources of information. But they face the same time limitations as everyone else. Further, few POs are master of all the skills they may need (that is almost impossible!). When this happens, it can make sense to split the role in two (Figure 19-2).

Strategic Product Owner
SPO

Tactical Product Owner
TPO

Figure 19-2. Strategic and Tactical Product Owner

One person, the SPO (Strategic Product Owner), looks at the long term; they focus on customers and strategy. The other, the TPO (Tactical Product Owner), focuses on the near term (this sprint, the next sprint, the next quarter). The TPO spends most of their time with the delivery team, while the SPO spends most of their time with customers and senior stakeholders.

The key thing about the SPO/TPO model is that the two people who hold the role need to speak with one voice. If they do not, then the model will fail. Ideally the SPO will stand in when the TPO is unavailable and vice versa.

The SPO/TPO model brings a number of benefits; it can also be used in several variations depending on the particular situation.

Scaling up

The SPO/TPO model is a first step in scaling up a team. As a team grows, delivery capacity increases, so a PO needs to feed more work into the team. If they lack time to understand and evaluate work, then the value of work being delivered may well fall.

When the technical team are well versed in the application domain, they may well be able to help the PO. But when the team lack application domain knowledge, they will require more information and explanation from the PO.

Using an SPO/TPO model creates time because one PO is focused on the delivery team, while the other looks at customers. This is particularly true when the nature of the customer base—or organization—means the PO must undertake time-consuming travel.

Similarly using two POs allows a greater range of skills and experience to be brought to bear on a problem—which again helps scaling-up. When a product has a large customer base, or hopes to have a large customer base, POs require more commercial skills. Again, the SPO/TPO model helps because one PO can be more commercially oriented, while the other focuses on the team.

TPO as proxy

Product Owners often lack the required time because they have another job to do. While the PO role is a full-time job, sometimes the person who is the right person to hold the role—usually because they command authority or knowledge—needs to combine the work with another role.

For example, on a financial trading desk the Product Owner may well be the senior trader. The trader knows both the domain and has the authority to say Yes or No to features. But by definition such a person lacks time. Normally I'd want a dedicated Product Owner in place, but sometimes the only way to have the necessary knowledge or authority is to have another job.

And sometimes the person who should be Product Owner—think our trader again—lacks the skills and experience to do the role. So again, they need help.

Multiple products

There are other occasions when the SPO/TPO model can be useful: big teams and multiple products.

Ideally there is one PO, one team, and one stream of work. But sometimes there are several products, teams, and streams. Here you might have an SPO who looks at the long term and several TPOs (Figure 19-3), each of whom works with one team on one stream.

Figure 19-3. Strategic Product Owner with multiple Tactical Product Owners

At this point I always think of Microsoft Office—although to be honest, I have no idea whatsoever how the Office team arrange themselves. I imagine on Strategic Product Owner for the Office product with several Tactical Product Owners for Word, Excel, PowerPoint, and so on.

The challenge with most software products—especially as they grow larger—is to find the splits that make both commercial sense and architectural sense. Large code bases are more difficult to work with, and larger code bases require more developers, and as teams get large, productivity falls off. But if teams are split without careful thought, they get in each other's way.

Downsides

As with all good patterns, the SPO/TPO model is not without its downsides, some perceived, some real.

I've heard Scrum advocates argue against this model: *One True Product Owner* they say. And they have a point putting more people between the delivery team and the customer does detract from communication.

One of the problems software development has traditionally faced is when multiple people think they have the right to say what is built next. Another problem occurs when the customer is remote from the development team and multiple people mediate what is asked for. When this happens One True Product Owner is a good solution.

But then the One True Product Owner can themselves become a bottleneck. Every time another link—another person—is introduced between the coders and the customer, the greater the propensity to introduce problems. More people mean more communication is needed, overheads increase, and the possibility of miscommunication or disagreement increases.

Another problem occurs when the person designated SPO is really a "Vanity SPO." This happens when someone covets the Product Owner position but is unsuitable to be the Product Owner. They may lack the skills, time, attention to detail, or understanding of the process. Rather than upset this person, they are given a suitably grand title—like "Strategic Product Owner"—and formal position. but all the work is actually done by someone else, the "de facto PO." In effect the team route around a problem.

This can be a great improvement for teams, but it also creates conditions for problems when the Vanity SPO realizes what is happening or simply starts asking for things the de facto PO doesn't think should be done or has told the team not to do.

Too many cooks

At the start of this chapter, I wrote: "Having a designated, and skilled, Product Owner can be a great step forward for many teams."

Then I explained how having two Product Owners—an SPO and a TPO—can be even better! So, the natural question is: *Could three Product Owners be even better? Or four? Or five?*

Maybe, but probably not.

When there is one person, there is no communication problem because everything is in one person's head. This is great but creates other problems, so a Product Owner is introduced which solves some of the other problems but introduces communication overheads and the risk of miscommunication.

When the PO role is split as an SPO and TPO, there are now two people between the customer and the developer. This deals with some problems but adds to the communication overheads. Every extra person between the customer and the developer magnifies communication problems and increases the risk of absent or miscommunication (Figure 19-4).

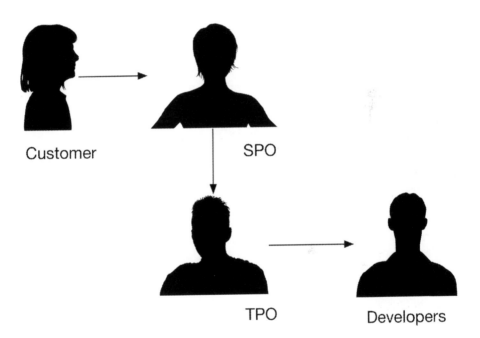

Figure 19-4. Two Product Owners between customer and developer

If two are not enough, then what about three? Or four?—Figure 19-5.

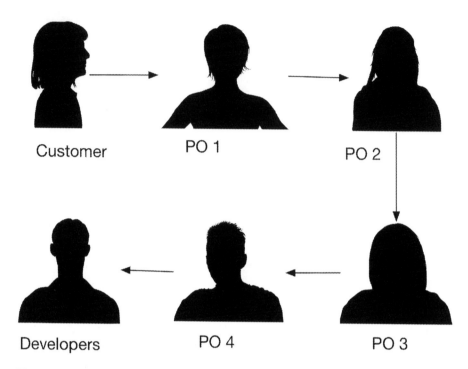

Figure 19-5. Four Product Owners between customer and developer

Every time another person is placed in the chain between customer(s) and Programmer, communication is impeded, slowed, facts can be lost, or misunderstandings and false beliefs added. Anyone who has ever played the party game of "telephone" or "Chinese whispers" should recognize the situation.

Indeed, in the pre-agile days, it was not uncommon to find long chains of Business Analysts talking to Business Analysts talking to Business Analysts. Actually, it is worse than this because many of the "conversations" are actually paper hand-offs. This still exists in some companies, especially those engaged in offshore outsourcing.

So, it comes down to a balance. When do the forces pushing toward having another intermediary outweigh those pushing to keep the chain short?

Or, to put it another way: When does adding another person to the chain improve matters more than the cost of adding another person?

For me the default answer is: there should be one Product Owner.

Going from none to one is a trade-off which often—but not always—makes sense. Going from one to two frequently makes sense but not always. Going from two to three...

Sometimes I can see a good case for having two: one Strategic and one Tactical, and perhaps multiple tactical Product Owners if the structure is right.

But having three people in the chain... I'm not saying never, but I do need convincing.

Four people in the chain... I find it hard to imagine ever being convinced here.

Product Council

If there really are so many people who need to have a say, perhaps the answer is not a chain but a committee. Perhaps all these people are really just important stakeholders. Perhaps what is needed here is one Product Owner with the legitimacy to take ideas and requests of multiple stakeholders and decide what is the right thing.

Sometimes this model is formalized with a Product Council (Figure 19-6). Such a council recognizes the importance of key stakeholders, those who have more of a say in the product direction than the average stakeholder. The council might contain internal and external stakeholders including actual customers. This provides a forum for different stakeholders to discuss what the product needs to do and options (including plans) for action.

Product Council

Product Owner

Figure 19-6. Product Council advises and reviews the work of the Product Owner

The council works in a number of ways. The Product Owner can talk informally to council members, develop one-on-one relationships, understand their concerns and needs in greater depth.

Sitting as a product board (like a company board of directors) provides a formal occasion for discussion between different interests. The board also provides a setting for Product Owners to report progress and present their view of future work and strategy.

A reoccurring solution

Lots of companies implement the SPO/TPO model with realizing that it is a reoccurring solution, a pattern. Each company thinks it is their own unique solution and gives the SPO and TPO roles their own names.

The model is not unique and deserves to be better known. Many more companies would benefit from adopting this model. Specifically, as I've already mentioned, there is a lot of work for a Product Owner to do, and one way of doing this is to share the load while also bringing more skills into play.

The job titles given to the SPO and TPO are unimportant. The Strategic Product Owner and Tactical Product Owner titles could be used; SPOs are sometimes called Product Managers, while TPOs get called Business Analysts (or Product Owners which is unfortunate).

Nor is it important exactly which person takes on which responsibilities. After all, some people are good at one thing and it makes sense to exploit that strength. Other times those who are less experienced in some aspect may positively want to get more experience. As long as the two individuals agree how they split the work up, things should work out.

Changing Hats

They always say that time changes things, but you actually have to change them yourself.

—Andy Warhol, American Artist (1928–1987)[1]

Being a Product Owner may be a calling, but it is seldom a first job. I have yet to meet a Product Owner who has not moved into the role from a related position. Product Owners can come from almost anywhere, but overwhelmingly they either have history with a product they own or a similar product.

A few Product Owners are from support, consulting, or training roles. After years of helping clients use the product, they transition to direct product development.

A sizeable number of Product Owners are former Business Analysts. This creates a quandary: Where does Business Analysis stop and product ownership begin? How should they change their approach?

Frankly, if you are moving from a Business Analysis to a Product Owner role, I wouldn't worry about such questions. The roles are similar enough that the experience carries over. I expect most of the changes will revolve around the scope and authority of the role. POs need to think more widely than BAs, specifically for commercial products—the market and competitors.

Another large group of Product Owners have been Product Managers. Again, I wouldn't worry about this transition; the roles are very similar. So similar

---

[1] Andy Warhol, *The Philosophy of Andy Warhol* (Penguin Classics, 2007).

© Allan Kelly 2019
A. Kelly, *The Art of Agile Product Ownership*,
https://doi.org/10.1007/978-1-4842-5168-3_20

that in many cases I think the change is little more than a change of title (and actually, I prefer the Product Manager title myself).

If you are transitioning from BA or Product Manager to Product Owner, I suggest you ask those around you how their expectations differ when you take off your old hat and put on the Product Owner hat.

In my experience, more Product Owners have a background as a software engineer, or Programmer, than anything else. In many organizations there is a belief that star coders make good Product Owners. Such a change can even be seen as a promotion - or the first move into management.

As someone who transitioned from programming to product management, I know such a change can be welcome and rewarding. When you have cared passionately about a product at the code level, it can be exciting to take on a product role directing the future of the product.

But such a transition can be problematic.

The same passion that enthuses you to be a good product champion when coding may be the same passion which blinds you to necessary changes. The best Product Owners are not necessarily those with the strongest and clearest vision of the product, but rather those who are most flexible in achieving their vision. Once you step away from the code and start talking to customers, those changes which looked obvious may look dangerous.

As a coder one lives the code, the detail, one empathizes with the code. Code speaks to you and you feel pain in the code. As a Product Owner sometimes you need to say, "I know this is a bad technical decision but full speed ahead and damn the torpedoes." (Although say this too often and the PO will torpedo themselves.)

Product Owners need to empathize with users and customers. Product Owners don't ignore technical considerations, but delivering for customers and creating value are the priority.

A coder moving to a product role needs to leave the Programmer hat behind and trust the technical team rather than second guess them. Indeed, there are few things worse than a Product Owner who writes technical stories directing the team on changes but does not describe what the change means to customers. Such stories undermine the responsibility of the technical experts doing the coding.

At an individual level, moving from code to product means embracing a personal change. Keeping one foot in the code camp makes the change more difficult. The best advice is to step away from the keyboard and cease coding.

Leaving one's old identity behind is impossible if a coder tries to be a part-time Product Owner and still spend time coding. Product Owner time is short enough as it is, and combining the role with another—like coding, support or product training—is harder still. Maintaining two identities, two focuses, and thought streams is nigh impossible.

This problem affects teams who practice collective team-based product ownership rather than centralizing the role. Individuals will be split between what the code wants and what the customer wants. Consequently, collective team-based product ownership is seldom effective.

Start-ups with limited staffing suffer from similar problems. Founders in particular seek to understand customers while maintaining their code output. Such problems may be hard to avoid in a start-up environment but that does not mean this approach should be recommended.

Unfortunately, the nature of the change from code to product is not always appreciated by organizations. It is common to hear talk of "Technical Product Owners." Such Product Owners invariably have a coding background and fill a quasi-architect role. They are neither one thing nor the other. They may talk the language of User Stories and value, but every decision is run through their own technical filters.

When organizations consider the role like this, they undermine the authority of the Product Owner. Invariably such people are not true owners—let alone entrepreneurs. Rather they are an administrative role which reports to another business-oriented role such as sales.

Commercial decisions—and authority—always trump technical decisions. One can dislike it as much as one likes but it is universally true even if it shouldn't be. Indeed, if technical arguments regularly win over commercial arguments, the business may not be around much longer.

It is certainly true that commercial people need to have a greater appreciation of the nature of software development and should learn more about technical issues. But it is even more beholden on technical staff to learn to put their arguments in commercial terms and explain why what is good for the code is good for the business.

This is where a coder turned Product Owner can excel. An appreciation of technical issues and opportunities allows Product Owners to see commercial opportunities with customers.

Mission Impossible

The perfect Product Owner probably doesn't exist. The role is hard to fill at the best of times. Frequently things are made more difficult by the constraints and extra demands organizations impose. That does not mean that one should give up trying, nor does it mean that one cannot be a good Product Owner.

It helps if one understands some of the potential conflicts and tensions inherent in the Product Owner role—if only so you don't feel alone! More importantly, if you know some of the potential pitfalls, you might be able to avoid them.

Skills

Look again at the Product Owner skills diagram (Figure 21-1). *What other skills would you add here?*

© Allan Kelly 2019
A. Kelly, *The Art of Agile Product Ownership*,
https://doi.org/10.1007/978-1-4842-5168-3_21

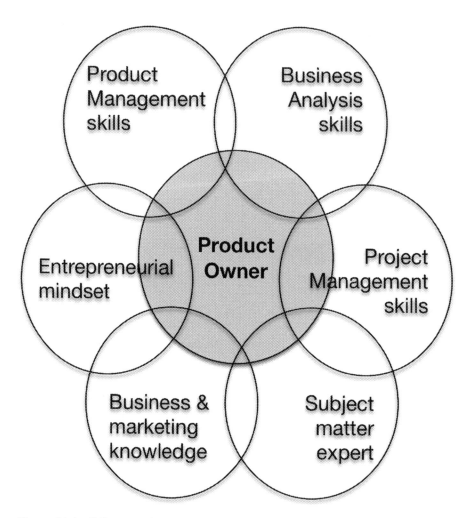

Figure 21-1. Skills required by Product Owners

At the very least, you will want to add Scrum and agile. Product Owners need to understand how agile methods work. I expect you will want to add a few more: inter personal skills, time management, political awareness—the list is endless.

The shear mix of skills a Product Owner might need is itself a source of tension. Few individuals will be expert in all such skills. Fortunately, few Product Owners need to be expert at everything. The exact mix of skills, and the depth of each, will vary from assignment to assignment.

Although that itself is a mixed blessing: while it means that no one needs to be an expert at everything, it means that the skills required in one PO role are not the same as another PO role. Someone who is a brilliant PO in one context might find that in another place they are running to catch up.

Product Owners need to be aware of the skills that vary from role to role. They need to ask themselves: "Do I have the right mix?" and "What additional skills do I need?" and "Which do I need to improve?"

In many ways it would be simpler if the Product Owner role was differentiated with different titles:

- Product Manager Owner: A commercial, market-oriented PO

- Business Analyst Owner: An internal process–oriented PO

- Project Manager Owner: A "deliver-all-this-stuff" type of PO

- Entrepreneur Product Owner: "I'm going to build this"

Yet, even though differentiating Product Owner roles like this would clarify expectations, it would create another set of problems. Organizations would create yet another set of job descriptions and role silos. Individuals would, by defining themselves as one type of Product Owner, exclude themselves from others. Rather than being a dynamic skill set, adjusting to circumstances, Product Owner skills would become ridgedly alinged with specific job titles.

So, despite the messiness that comes with a broad definition of Product Owner, and despite the burden it places on individuals to define the role for themselves, I would rather embrace the board definition and permeable role boundaries. Ultimately, the Product Owner needs to do what is needed to further the product rather than restrict themselves to a narrow set of activities contained in a role definition.

Authority

The Product Owner struggles with authority on many levels. As already mentioned, the organization concerned may place limits on the PO; they may expect the PO to play second fiddle to a Product Manager or Project Manager.

When an organization defines the PO role narrowly ("deliver this backlog"), the role is constrained, and many approaches and tools are unavailable. Conversely when an organization defines the role very broadly ("go discover and deliver a product"), the amount of work increases.

Even within the team, POs can struggle with authority. If they are not seen as the legitimate PO by other team members, their authority will be limited.

To complicate matters, there is a potential conflict within Scrum itself:

> Scrum Teams are self-organizing and cross-functional. Self-organizing teams choose how best to accomplish their work, rather than being directed by others outside the team. (Scrum Guide[1])

And later, on the same page:

> The Product Owner is the sole person responsible for managing the Product Backlog. Product Backlog management includes:
>
> • Clearly expressing Product Backlog items;
>
> • Ordering the items in the Product Backlog to best achieve goals and missions

In effect Scrum says, "the team are all equals and self-organize to deliver the best result" but also says "the Product Owner is responsible for deciding what the team will do." While many teams find no conflict in this, there are those that do.

Certainly, Schwaber and Sutherland did not intend there to be conflict, but the potential is there. When Product Owners are outside the team, there is greater potential conflict. But even when the PO is a team member, the "first among equals" status can cause difficulties.

Individual level

Authority issues can play out at an individual level too. A PO may find it hard to know when to ask the team to do something and when to leave them to self-organization. The PO may hold back when they should lead, or lead when they should let go.

Although the PO is—or at least should be—a team member, they may well find themselves isolated because their role, and skills, makes them different from other team members. Some differences of opinion are almost inevitable because the PO represents "the business" and the delivery team "the technology." One hopes these are creative tensions, but each has the potential to be difficult.

Within the organization it can be hard for individuals to know how far they can go. When companies start talking about self-organization and devolving the authority downward, old hands frequently become cynical. Every instance

---

[1] Schwaber and Sutherland, "The Scrum Guide: The Definitive Guide to Scrum."

of management action not matching words are seen a proof that "they" don't mean what they say.

The same issue manifests itself when dealing with customers. POs will feel pressure to deliver what customers want when they are face to face with that customer—everyone likes to say "Yes." But they may know that commercially what this customer is asking for is not a priority.

Misunderstanding the role

The Product Owner is a relatively new role, and although on paper the responsibilities of one PO may look similar to those of another ("understand what the customer wants, capture ideas in the backlog, and prioritize work for the team"), how those responsibilities are executed hides massive variations.

So, it should come as little surprise that organizations, teams, and individuals understand, and misunderstand, the PO role. Perhaps the most common misunderstanding is to see the PO as a type of Project Manager. As pointed out earlier, there is a fundamental difference in the two roles:

- Project Managers are predominantly concerned with the "when." They regard the "what" as defined, their job is to deliver it.

- Product Owners are predominantly concerned with the "what." For a PO, the "when" is one of several variables which influence the value delivered.

Of course, a Project Manager is but one type of manager. POs are mistaken for other types of manager too. In fact, given that companies transforming to agile self-organization remove managers in general, POs can be seen as "the last manager standing." Even though they lack the term "manager" in their title, like a Scrum Master, they are "non-commissioned managers."

As such companies sometimes add extra responsibilities to the PO which are not found in the books, risk and resource management are common. When companies make POs line managers of team members, a whole host of potential conflicts arise.

The problem with these extra responsibilities is that it compounds all the other problems: POs need even more skills; their authority position is confused further and worst of all: they have less time.

Time

Time is probably the biggest problem Product Owner face. Companies can give POs more staff, more money, and more perks but they cannot give a PO more time. Even the most senior, most successful PO has the same number of hours in a day as you or me: 24.

The larger a team is and the more customers a product has, the greater the work a PO needs to do. There are ways of supporting the PO and dividing the role, but each of these comes at a cost: communication. The more people support the PO, the more time a PO needs to spend in communication.

As discussed in earlier chapters, while POs need to share responsibility, they also need to say no and turn push back on some requests to do more work.

Recognizing the tensions

One day organizations might understand the Product Owner role; organizations and the community will recognize different types of Product Owner and the accompanying skillsets. With understanding will come appropriate levels of authority and support. Taken together Product Owners will be able to have a more normal work life.

Until that day comes, every PO needs to recognize the tensions inherent in their role and present in their organization. Recognizing those tensions may not remove the tensions, but it should allow a degree of management.

Recognizing and managing those tensions on a case by case basis goes hand in hand with the central argument of this book: every Product Owner must make the role their own.

The End

As I near the end, let me return to that challenge I posed in the introduction of this book:

What is the best way for you to fill the Product Owner role?

Only you can answer this question. I have my own ideas, yours are probably different. If you look closely I am sure you will find I contradict myself at times. You will find that even your Product Owner colleagues have, at least, a slightly different take. Even those employed in the same organization as yourself, with the same role and responsibility description, will differ.

Product Owner maturity model

In Chapter 17, I described the Business Analysis maturity model (Figure 17-3) from Debra Paul and Assist KD. This model can be repurposed for the Product Owner (Figure 22-1).

© Allan Kelly 2019
A. Kelly, *The Art of Agile Product Ownership*,
https://doi.org/10.1007/978-1-4842-5168-3_22

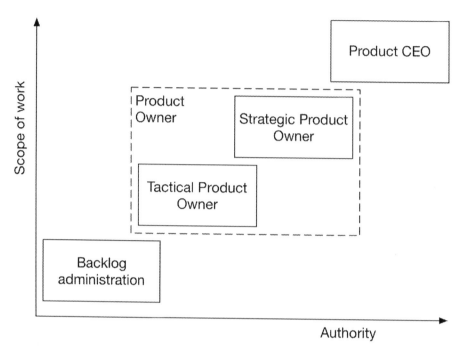

Figure 22-1. Product ownership maturity model

As an individual you might almost see this as a career model:

As a newly appointed Product Owner, your job is to review and edit the backlog, refine the stories, and write acceptance criteria. Every 2 weeks you select a few stories and run them past your superiors. When they have agreed, you can take them to the team who will load them into a sprint.

With time you grow in experience and authority; your superiors are happy for you to select the stories yourself. They trust you to create rolling quarter plans of what is coming up and enquire with customers as to their expectations. But they retain strategy.

Success allows your authority to grow; you meet more customers, talk to more people in your own company, clock up the frequent flyer points, and start to influence strategy. One day you find you are leading strategy. You might still be working with the team or you might have someone else to do that.

In time you become a mini-CEO, you are involved with negotiations with customers, suppliers, legal people, and finance. The issues aren't so black and white at this level, and you probably still have an actual CEO—and others—to answer to.

Alternatively you might view this model as the journey of an organization:

In the beginning the company adopts Scrum and so need Product Owners. These Product Owners lack real power so spend their days reviewing the backlog, adding stories they are told to add, editing existing stories, writing acceptance criteria, and feeding the development team.

As the organization as a whole becomes more agile, more authority is delegated down the hierarchy. Product Owners are now able to plan work for the sprint without checking with superiors and in time can create draft plans for future sprints.

More authority is delegated and those doing the work need to meet customers, come up with visions, and generally create a strategy.

In time the agile organization moves from the hierarchical model to an Amoeba management model with multiple independent business units producing their own plans and executing on those plans to maximize value.

The challenge for Product Owners is not just to define their own role and find their own way. The challenge is to grow as Product Owners as the organization itself grows, matures, and, hopefully, becomes more agile.

Amoeba management originated at Kyocera Corporation and is described by Kazuo Inamora in *Amoeba Management*.[1] My book *Continuous Digital*[2] describes the model applied to software teams.

Final words

Ultimately Product Owners derive their authority and legitimacy from their skills and their contact with customers. They may, in the first instance, derive authority because they are appointed to the role. But a position on an organizational hierarchy chart counts for little in a self-organizing, cross-skilled, high-performing team.

Product Owners need a wide variety of specialist skills and expertise. That knowledge gives them the authority to determine what the delivery team is going to build.

---

[1] K. Inamori, *Amoeba Management* (CRC Press—Taylor Francis Group, 2013).
[2] Allan Kelly, *Continuous Digital* (Software Strategy Ltd / LeanPub, 2018), https://leanpub.com/cdigital/.

All POs need the skills of listening, enquiry, analysis, and understanding. More needed skills come from Product Management and Business Analysis domains. There are other skills too: POs must be commercially savvy, understand business strategy, have domain knowledge, understand elements of project and general management, and more.

The exact mix of skills needed by each Product Owner will vary. Often a Product Owner will need to acquire new skills and knowledge on the job. They need to draw on the skills, knowledge, and experience of others.

Many organizations and Product Owners define the role narrowly. In this book I encourage you to define the role more broadly. That comes at a cost, but, ultimately, I think it makes for better teams and better products and, far more importantly, is personally more satisfying.

R

References

Alexander, I., and L. Beus-Dukic. *Discovering Requirements*. Chichester: John Wiley & Sons, 2009.

Beck, K. *Extreme Programming Explained*. Addison-Wesley, 2000.

Blank, S. *The Four Steps to Epiphany*. K&S Ranch, 2013.

Brooks, F. *The Mythical Man Month: Essays on Software Engineering*. Addison-Wesley, 1975.

Cagan, M. *Inspired: How to Create Products Customers Love*. SVPG Press, 2008.

Christensen, C. M., S. C. Anthony, G. Berstell, and D. Nitterhouse. "Finding the Right Job For Your Product." *Sloan Management Review* 48, no. 3 (Spring 2007): 38–47.

Christensen, C. M. *Competing against Luck*. Harper Collins, 2016.

Drucker, P. F. *The Age of Discontinuity*, 1969.

Drucker, P. F. *The Practice of Management*. Harper & Row, 1954.

Gilb, T. *Competitive Engineering*. Butterworth-Heinemann, 2005.

Inamori, K. *Amoeba Management*. CRC Press—Taylor Francis Group, 2013.

Jones, C. *Applied Software Measurement*. McGraw Hill, 2008.

Jones, C., B. Bonsignour, and J. Subramanyam. *The Economics of Software Quality*. Addison-Wesley, 2011.

Kelly, A. *Business Patterns for Software Developers*. Chichester: John Wiley & Sons, 2012.

Kelly, A. *Continuous Digital*. Software Strategy Ltd / LeanPub, 2018. `https://leanpub.com/cdigital/`.

Kelly, A. *Project Myopia*. Software Strategy Ltd / LeanPub, 2018.

© Allan Kelly 2019
A. Kelly, *The Art of Agile Product Ownership*,
https://doi.org/10.1007/978-1-4842-5168-3

Lash, J. P. *Helen and Teacher: The Story of Helen Keller and Anne Sullivan Macy.* Delacorte Press/Seymour Lawrence, 1980.

Martin, A., R. Biddle, and J. Noble. "The XP Customer Role in Practice: Three Studies," 2004.

Martin, D. N. *In Misbehave: Speak Truth to Power.* Inkwater Press, 2011.

Moore, G. A. *Crossing the Chasm.* Capstone publishing, 1999.

Office of Government Commerce. *Tailoring PRINCE2.* London: TSO (The Stationary Office), 2002.

Parnas, D. L., and Clements, P. C. "A Rational Design Process: How and Why to Fake It." *IEEE Transactions on Software Engineering* 12, no. 2 (1986): 251–57.

Parnas, D. L., and Clements, P. C. "A Rational Design Process: How and Why to Fake It." In *Software Fundamentals: Collected Papers of David L. Parnas*, edited by D. M. and Weiss Hoffman. Addison-Wesley, 2001.

Patton, J. "Dual Track Development Is Not Duel Track." *Dual Track Development Is Not Duel Track* (blog). Accessed 30 June 2018. https://jpattonassociates.com/dual-track-development/.

Paul, D. and D. Yates, eds. *Business Analysis.* The British Computer Society, 2006.

Reed, A. "It's Time to Ditch the Bridge," April 21, 2016. https://www.adrianreed.co.uk/2016/04/21/its-time-to-ditch-the-bridge/.

Ries, E. *The Lean Startup.* Crown Publishing Group, 2011.

Schwaber, K., and M. Beedle. *Agile Software Development with Scrum.* Addison-Wesley, 2002.

Schwaber, K, and Jeff Sutherland. "The Scrum Guide: The Definitive Guide to Scrum," 2017. https://www.scrumguides.org/download.html.

Verganti, R. *Overcrowded.* MIT Press, 2016.

Warhol, A. *The Philosophy of Andy Warhol.* Penguin Classics, 2007.

Index

Printed in the United States
By Bookmasters